D0207932

DISCOVERING THE

OKANAGAN

DISCOVERING THE

OKANAGAN

the ultimate guide

JIM COUPER

whitecap

The information in this book is true and complete to the best of our knowledge.
All recommendations are made without guarantee on the part of the author or
Whitecap Books Ltd. The author and publisher disclaim any liability in connection
with the use of this information.
For additional information, please contact Whitecap Books Ltd.,
351 Lynn Avenue, North Vancouver, BC v7J 2C4.
Visit our web site at www.whitecap.ca

Edited by Elaine Jones
Proofread by Andrea Scott-Bigsby
Cover design by Stacey Noyes
Cover photograph by Alan Hoffman
Art direction by Roberta Batchelor
Interior design by Margaret Lee / www.bamboosilk.com
Photographs by Jim Couper unless otherwise specified
Map by Jacqui Thomas

Printed and bound in Canada

Thanks to Kelly Reid at Tourism Development Services in Penticton, Big White Ski
Resort and Apex Mountain Resort for the use of several colour and black and white
photographs.

NATIONAL LIBRARY OF CANADA CATALOGUING IN PUBLICATION DATA

Couper, Jim
    Discovering the Okanagan / Jim Couper.

Includes bibliographical references and index.
ISBN 1-55285-588-0

    1. Okanagan River Valley (B.C. and Wash.)--Guidebooks.
I. Title.

FC3845.04A3 2004   917.11'5   C2004-902780-8

The publisher acknowledges the support of the Canada Council for the Arts and the
Cultural Services Branch of the Government of British Columbia for our publishing pro-
gram. We acknowledge the financial support of the Government of Canada through the
Book Publishing Industry Development Program for our publishing activities.

To my wife Lian, for her support, encouragement, editing suggestions, ideas and endless enthusiasm for the many excursions, both in the Okanagan and abroad.

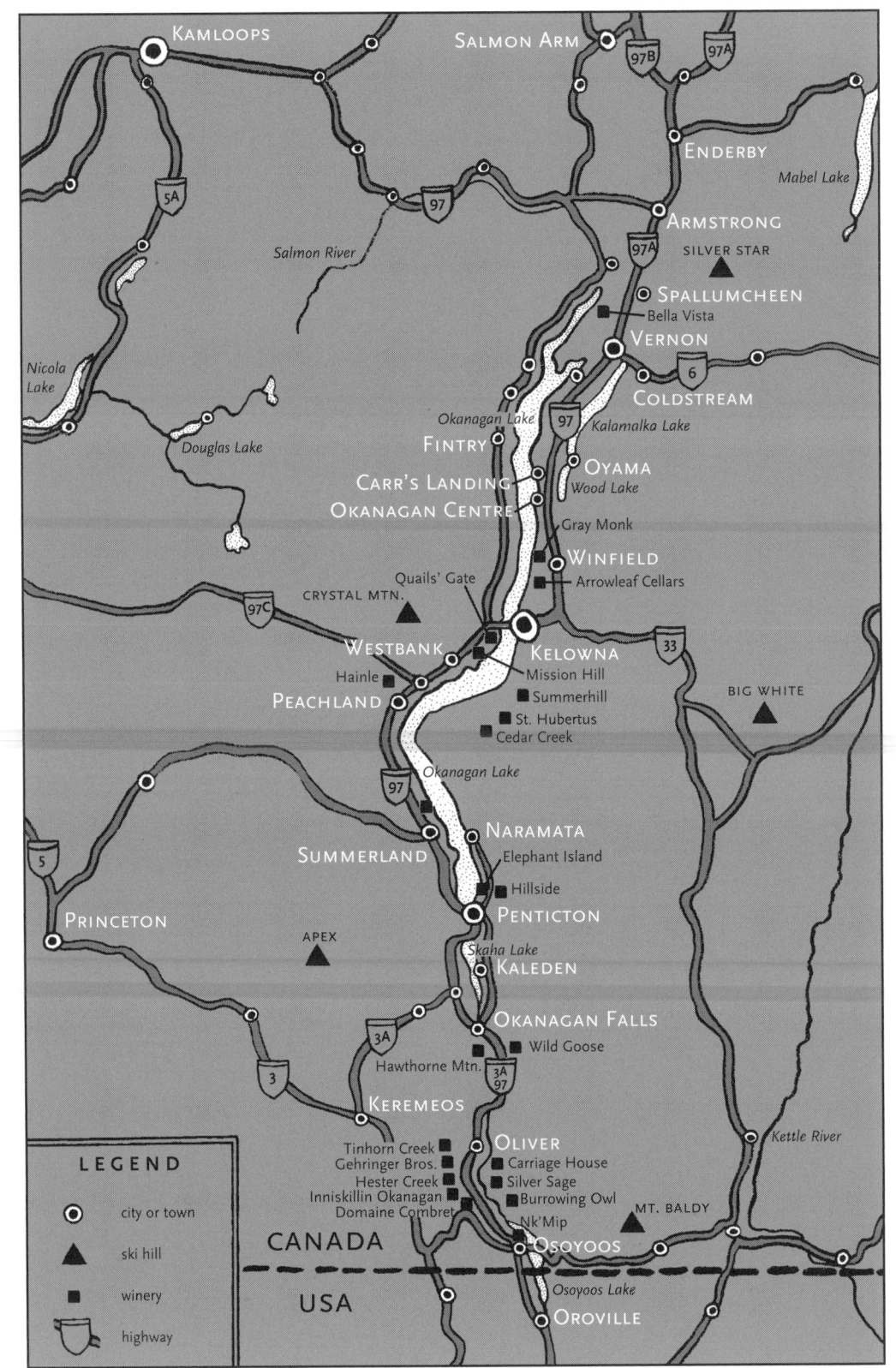

THE READ AHEAD

3 FEATURE PRESENTATIONS OF THE OKANAGAN   99
   Wine and Wineries   99
   Dining and Entertainment at Wineries   102
   Wine Events   103
   Biking and Hiking, Walking and Jogging   105
   Skiing and Boarding   115
   Golf in the Valley   122
   Okanagan Wildlife   127
   Wildlife Viewing and Nature Preserves   133
   Festivals, Fairs and Annual Events   140
   Okanagan, B.C. Calendar of Events   140
   Okanogan, Washington Calendar of Events   155

4 FOR MORE INFORMATION   159
   Books   159
   Tourist Information Centres   161

INDEX   163

ACKNOWLEDGEMENTS

On starting this book I had no thoughts of contacting the local tourist bureaus since I knew the Valley well and thought I needed no help. Then I came upon a minor roadblock and fired off an email to a tourism office with a question and a brief explanation. I got an immediate answer, an offer of help for other endeavors and the path was cleared to such a degree that I contacted the tourism offices and Chambers of Commerce in every Valley community. Since I care about how the Okanagan is presented to the world, I was curious about the degree of professionalism that would be shown here, at home. To my relief it was, with one exception, first class. For their effort I thank Pat Burns and Tommi Hanley in Kelowna, Kelly Reid in Penticton, Gary and Carol Mathers in Oliver and Michelle Jefferson in Osoyoos.

Deserving of special appreciation are family members Archie, Florence, Dylan, Jillian, Dawn, Marlene, Ron, Hayley, Jason and Loretta.

Herb Isaac shared with us his love and passion for the Okanagan, his native land.

An Independent Approach

This book was written without any financial contribution from any government agency, arts council or foundation. The information presented here is uncontaminated by editorial slant and the opinions expressed, no matter how obtuse, are mine and belong to no one else. I have visited all the attractions listed and have eaten in all the restaurants that are described. Sometimes I paid my own way and sometimes I was a guest. There are close to 1,000 eateries in the Okanagan, yet this book mentions only a few dozen. The criteria for inclusion are most, if not all, of the following: an atmosphere that is in some way unique, longevity, an interesting attribute and a reputation for good food.

A final acknowledgement goes to KOA campgrounds, which allowed us to stay, at no charge, at its facilities while preparing this book.

Feedback about this book can be directed to the publisher or to okedits@hotmail.com.

AUTHOR'S PREAMBLE

In 1977, along with my wife, Lian, and three-year-old son, Dylan, I departed Toronto, not just to see the world, but also to see if there was a better place in which to live than Canada, the country my parents had deposited me in, at age three, when they left their Scottish homeland. After travelling for 16 months in 60 or so countries and claiming the title "only people to have reached the ends of the Earth's most northerly and most southerly roads in the same vehicle," we returned home.

Despite the beauty of Nepal, the climate of Ecuador, the gregariousness of the Argentines, the culture of Europe and the soul of India, the odyssey ended right where it began. Southern Ontario looked clean, vibrant and hospitable — a wonderful place in which to live.

In 1980 we four (daughter Jillian had been born) were ensconced in the middle of the Niagara Peninsula, a plane enhanced by an escarpment, bordered by two of the Great Lakes and cut by a big gorge with a famous waterfall. It is a revered spot in Canada with a relatively moderate climate that supports grapes, cherries and peaches.

For 15 years we house-hopped until we landed in a modest home on a country acre overlooking a golf course and a winding river. When the United Nations repeatedly named Canada the best country in which to live, we knew we had the best of the best. We looked from the top of the Niagara Escarpment out across the clear waters of Lake Ontario and our gaze reached beyond the curvature of the Earth, encompassed all that we knew and ended with a self-congratulatory pat on the back.

There was but one nagging doubt. On several automobile trips around North America Lian and I had become enchanted with a long, lovely, lake-filled valley in the western Canadian mountains. Our three-year itch to move was needing scratching. But any further relocation could be regressive. Normally we move at the drop of a key, but with a deed on the best spot in the best country we knew we would never find as good a location if we returned, disappointed. So we did something we had never done — a preliminary study, a reconnaissance: a six-week trip to the Okanagan.

Expectations are always dangerous and if the Valley didn't match our embellished memories and enhanced anticipations, it wasn't its fault. Yes, it was an extremely nice place. A little brown in August perhaps, but at least the sun always shone and it was hard not be awed by a panorama of mountains and lakes. As in Niagara, grapes, peaches and other tender fruit did well. Even kiwis grew. But, of course, it was short of Utopia and not quite Eden, although crossing the mountains and entering the Valley was reminiscent of Ronald Colman discovering Shangri-La in the 1937 movie, Lost Horizon.

Real estate was 50 percent pricier than at home, unemployment was high, and, judging by the sizes of the houses and cars, wealth was the norm. We feared we would not fit in.

Three tiny, inconsequential incidents, which in themselves meant nothing, established the tenor of the Valley and led us to our decision.

- In a parking lot two pre-teen boys raced their bicycles and knocked over a large garbage barrel, spilling its contents. Instead of riding on, as I expected, they dismounted, righted the bin and picked up every item of fetid refuse they had spilled.
- In a store I was discreetly reading a newspaper I didn't intend to purchase when a loud female voice demanded, "You gonna read that or you gonna buy it?" Caught unawares I fumbled for change while the clerk laughed and said, "Gotcha didn't I?" She insisted I take the paper outside, sit in the sun, read it and return it when I was through.
- At a gas station I asked for $20 worth. The attendant got side-tracked and didn't stop the pump until it read $21.20. As I felt in my pockets for the extra change he said, "Don't worry about it; doesn't matter." As we walked to the cash register I asked him about life in the Okanagan and his answer summed up the feelings I had about the pleasantness of the people, "We're pretty laid back here."

It took a year to sell our house and business, and the winter was spent crossing the southern United States and visiting some wonderful spots in Florida, Texas and California. Our son went ahead with his girlfriend to attend university in Vancouver and our teenage daughter travelled with us. We often talked of staying at places along the way but when we saw an ad in a Phoenix newspaper "Give a Gun For Christmas," we knew we would be moving on. Besides, it was our quest to find the best spot on the planet and the United Nations had declared that it must be in Canada.

We spent our life savings and became mortgage-bound with an enormous house in Kelowna that was really just average in size and price for the Okanagan. It sat on 2.5 beautiful hectares (6.5 acres) of steep hillside overlooking both valley and lake.

As we settled in, unexpected things happened. We quickly made friends — wonderful people made us part of their families and invited us into their circles of activities. Store clerks laughed and joked and asked questions. No one robotically mumbled, "Thank you for shopping at blah blah." We took up skiing — a sport we had abandoned because of high costs, long lift lines and short runs. We found that tennis nets remained up in winter and we could often play in December and January. We tried snowshoeing, sailing, orienteering and mountain climbing and also rediscovered fishing, hiking and mountain biking. The array of outdoor activities so amazed us that we started a magazine about health, ecology and participation sports and then had a new experience — business failure.

Despite that, the right decision had been made and the tranquil Valley, immune to the ravages of nature that shook the TV nightly, was our happy home. No earthquakes, hurricanes, tornadoes, mudslides, floods, ice storms, blizzards, avalanches or volcanoes threatened, although forest fire threats were sometimes a minor summer concern. That was the way it was until British Columbia's summer of flames when, in late August of 2003, the infamous Okanagan Mountain fire consumed 238 Kelowna homes and a winery, and caused the evacuation of 26,000 people. Also burned, in the hottest driest summer on record, were a dozen magnificent trestles of the historic Kettle Valley Rail Trail that took hikers and bikers through the mountains high above the Valley. We were fortunate to live in the part of the city most distant from the fire.

Our three-year itch to move has struck again and again, but there is nowhere to go: we know there is no better place to live.

When we settled in the Okanagan our insatiable quest for discovery continued and we obsessively explored every fascinating nook and cranny of the Valley. That spirit has led to this book and the pleasure of sharing our discoveries and rediscoveries. We hope it helps you to enjoy the best place on planet Earth in which to live.

Sunset over North Okanagan

1 THE WHERE AND WHAT OF THE OKANAGAN

There are many theories about the derivation of the name Okanagan, but most agree it comes from the Interior Salish language and contains the word head, as in the head of a river. One translation is *looking towards the head* while another offering is *seeing the head*. Still another says it refers to a point in the river near Okanagan Falls that is the head of the river, being as far as the salmon swim upstream. There are no fewer than 47 different recorded spellings of the name of the lake, the river, the mountain and the Valley. These include Lewis and Clark's Otchenaukane and David Thompson's Ookanawgan.

CLIMATE AND LOCATION

Okanagan summers are hot and endlessly sunny, while the cloudy winters are short and tranquil. In November and December of 2002 I shovelled snow from my driveway twice and in early 2003, just once.

When eastern friends ask for details about the climate here, I say there are five months of summer (May, June, July, August and September), two of autumn (October and November), three of winter (December, January and February) and two of spring (March and April). I may be exaggerating the length of winter, as autumn weather can extend into December and spring seems to start before the end of February. People from Winnipeg or Edmonton would probably say we have no winter at all. It's all relative, but it is a fact that in Oliver/Osoyoos, in the south of the Valley, a half-dozen recreational vehicle parks keep busy 12 months of the year and a golf course in Oliver stays open through the winter.

If the Okanagan was in the Yukon or northern Saskatchewan, there is no doubt it would still be a popular place, but the number of residents and visitors would be dramatically reduced. Fortunately it is in the very south of British Columbia with the 10th busiest airport in Canada connecting directly to major Canadian and American cities. By road it is a half day from Vancouver and close enough to Edmonton and Calgary to make it a summer vacation destination.

Sun and Rain in Central Okanagan

AVERAGE HOURS OF SUNLIGHT
January = 46 hrs.
July = 310 hrs.
Yearly Total = 2010 hrs.

PRECIPITATION
January = 3.2 cm (1.25 in.)
July = 2.35 cm (.95 in.)
Yearly Total = 31 cm (12.3 in.)

SNOWFALL
Yearly Total = 95 cm (37 in.)

OKANAGAN LITE:
Finding the Okanagan in Space

CAPTAIN: I'd like to visit the Okanagan next week.

NAVIGATOR: I'm sure you would sir, but it's unbelievably difficult to find.

CAPTAIN: I don't see why it should be, it's quite well known.

NAVIGATOR: As I recall it's in the Milky Way: a rather large spiral galaxy with two satellite galaxies.

CAPTAIN: So what's the problem?

NAVIGATOR: There are more than a billion galaxies, sir. And although less than one-third are spiral and not many have two satellites, we've really only narrowed it down to 100,000 possibilities.

CAPTAIN: But I want to go. The weather is delightful and you can ski, golf, play tennis, ice skate and water ski all on the same day.

NAVIGATOR: You're the boss and the Navitron can help us. Once we find the Milky Way we have to find the sun, Sol, among 100 billion stars. I believe it has nine planets, is at half-life, and is 30,000 light-years from the galaxy centre. If we should find Sol, we then have to find the third planet, Earth, and then find this Okanagan place.

CAPTAIN: That's where I come in. I know you look for the longest land mass that runs from one polar cap to another and has a saline solution on either side. On the side where the sun sets you locate the bottom-most of a series of large islands and then go inland on the continent about 1/12th of the way and stop when you come to a long stringy body of fresh water surrounded by mountains, with a semi-desert at the bottom.

NAVIGATOR: That's amazing captain. How do you know that?

CAPTAIN: I picked up a handy little guidebook when we stopped at Zoxeeg. It tells you everything you need to know. Set course for Earth.

EXTENT OF THE OKANAGAN VALLEY

Finding the Okanagan is not much of a problem. It's immediately north of the United States and 400 kilometres (250 miles) east of the Pacific Ocean. Determining where it begins and ends is much more demanding. The Okanagan that this book is about is not a political, jurisdictional or electoral area, therefore it does not have carefully marked boundaries. We are sticking to a geographical definition.

Most commonly it is considered to be the valley containing Okanagan Lake. Note that it is spelled with one O and three As. Once the valley that holds Okanagan Lake and Okanagan River crosses the 49th parallel and enters United States, the Okanagan does not stop but simply changes its name to Okanogan—two Os and two As. As far as we are concerned this is the same valley, although it is no longer the area around Okanagan Lake. For the purposes of this book, the Okanagan continues from just north of Armstrong to the point where the Okanogan River flows into the Columbia River in Washington State. That makes it a broad, hook-shaped trough occupied by a chain of lakes that first drain north—Duck, Wood and Kalamalka—and then south—Swan, Okanagan, Skaha, Vaseux and Osoyoos. The Valley covers roughly 10,000 square kilometres (3,860 square miles). That sounds like a lot but is really only an area slightly more than 32 kilometres (20 miles) wide and 305 kilometres (190 miles) long.

The exact extent of the Okanagan is something of a moot point because (with apologies to our American neighbours) there is much less interest in the sparsely populated area between Oroville (just south of Osoyoos) and Brewster, Washington, where the Okanagan waters merge with the Columbia River, than there is north of the international border. On the other hand, there is a great deal that is slightly north of the Okanagan boundary that is worthy of note.

Just outside of Armstrong (north of Vernon) a sign beside Highway 97 denotes the "Okanagan Great Divide." Rain that falls on the north side of this marker flows north towards Enderby and ends up in the Shuswap system, which flows into the Thompson River, then the Fraser River and then into the Pacific Ocean. It enters the salty brine about 350 kilometres (217 miles) north of rain that flows to the Pacific by way of the Columbia River.

A Raindrop's Journey

Let's follow a raindrop that falls on the south side of this divide. Assuming it doesn't evaporate in the summer sun or get slurped

Approximate Driving Distances to Kelowna

Calgary	502 kilometres (317 miles)
Edmonton	897 kilometres (538 miles)
Seattle	504 kilometres (302 miles)
Spokane	408 kilometres (245 miles)
Vancouver	395 kilometres (237 miles)

up by a thirsty cow, it will join its downpouring friends and form a rivulet that flows downhill and possibly ends up in BX Creek (named after Bernard Exchange where tired horses were exchanged for fresh ones). This flows into the south end of Swan Lake, a shallow natural habitat just north of Vernon. BX Creek enters Swan Lake very close to where it exits Swan Lake, which explains why there isn't much water flow in this shallow pond. Very slowly our raindrop will make its way down BX Creek and enter Vernon Creek, which flows into the north end of Okanagan Lake. There it begins a leisurely but delightful trip down the big lake, passing Fintry Delta, McKinley Landing and eventually flowing under the floating bridge at Kelowna.

Okanagan Lake is extremely deep and thus has a vast amount of water with only one small river/canal in the south end to drain it. The input is not extensive either. Mission Creek, which dries to a trickle in summer, is the largest water source. Imagine a huge swimming pool being drained through a straw: it takes 58 years before all the water — including our raindrop — is drained from the lake and new water replenishes it.

Many years later, after passing Peachland and Summerland and Naramata, our drop of moisture reaches Penticton and joins a throng of happy rafters and tubers who jump into the Okanagan River Channel and float along until they reach Skaha Lake about an hour later.

At the south end of Skaha Lake, at Okanagan Falls, our raindrop tumbles over a series of flood-control dams that supplant the original twin falls for which the town is named. It ends up in Vaseux Lake, a shallow, tranquil habitat where noisy boats with motors are prohibited. After slowly floating the length of this little lake with its myriad of wildlife, the Okanagan River, which is really a channel, takes over and flows past the town of Oliver and into Osoyoos Lake. The journey continues past the town of Osoyoos, under a small bridge and around a long peninsula that reaches into the lake and hosts Haynes Point Provincial Park. The Canada/U.S. border divides the lake and without so much as the show of a passport the raindrop becomes an American and then the lake narrows into its natural river shape. Here there are no channels and just one dam, so the Okanogan River meanders at will and drops about 30 metres (100 feet) on its way to join the mighty Columbia River, one of the biggest in the U.S.

Just before the town of Brewster, Washington, the relatively small Okanogan merges with the Columbia adding a little warmth to its cold flow. United they head for the Pacific.

A More Scenic Route

Should strong winds have taken the little cloud that held our raindrop slightly northeast of Kelowna, it might have fallen somewhere that would have made the journey much longer. A smaller three-lake valley runs parallel to and just 30 kilometres (19 miles) east of Okanagan Lake. It is the end of the hook shape that comprises the Okanagan Valley. If our wet globule fell near Kelowna's airport it would have been only a few kilometres from Okanagan Lake, through which it would eventually pass. Near where the airplanes land, a few streams flow into Duck Lake (also known as Ellison Lake), a shallow muddy refuge for aquatic birds and determined water skiers. From there it would have gone northward in Winfield Creek and flowed into Wood Lake and then through a short canal (that goes under a causeway) that leads into Kalamalka Lake. This lake drains into Vernon Creek, which connects with BX Creek on its way to the north end of Okanagan Lake, which takes us back to the original journey.

A VIEW THROUGH THE EYE OF TIME

I was going to head this introductory section "History of the Okanagan" but I could hear the yawns and I could imagine the book dropping to the floors of stores. History is sometimes a dirty word, synonymous with dull and boring. But you've started reading so you might as well continue — this will be short. It's the fat-free, lite version of what happened before you got here.

Dinosaurs and the Sex Lives of Neanderthals are not Applicable

I cannot titillate with tales of dinosaurs, or the intimate lives of Neanderthals, since neither chose to live here. Had they made better lifestyle decisions they could have lived happily ever after, instead of becoming extinct.

About two billion years before we celebrated the second millennium, the continent of North America wasn't as big as it is now. If people had lived in the Okanagan they would have had oceanfront views and the people in Vancouver would have been under a lot of salty water. The Okanagan was the continental shelf of a giant ocean and the sediment that settled to the floor was the origin of much of our rock. The oldest rock in B.C. is right here. McIntyre Bluff (between Oliver and Okanagan Falls) and the cliffs opposite the Bluff on the east side of Vaseux Lake are that very sediment that was metamorphosed into gneiss and schist 180 million years ago.

Not so very long ago — just 20 million years — it got hot here

A Road by Any Other Name

Highway 97 is the backbone of both the Canadian Okanagan and the American Okanogan, running from Brewster, Washington, to Vernon, B.C., and then to Kamloops. Although there is no shortage of names and numbers for highways, the province has chosen to confuse the situation by adding Highways 97A, 97B and 97C.

North of Vernon, Highway 97 curves to the west and the road that continues north is 97A. The main road that joins Westbank and Peachland is Highway 97, but the one that branches west to Vancouver is 97C. It also gets another name, The Connector. North of Enderby, 97B goes to Salmon Arm. Within the cities it travels through, Highway 97 usually gets a second name—such as Harvey Ave. in Kelowna, and Main St. in several other communities. Highway 97 is the longest north-south road in North America, stretching from the Yukon to California.

Okanagan Lake Measurements

SURFACE AREA
34,802 hectares
(135 square miles)

MAXIMUM DEPTH
244 metres (800 feet)

MAXIMUM WIDTH
4 kilometres (2.5 miles)

MINIMUM WIDTH
1.6 kilometres (1 mile)

LENGTH
145 kilometres (90 miles)

RENEWAL TIME
58 years

and volcanoes spewed lava and ash and filled the Valley with hot smelly stuff. Mt. Boucherie in Westbank and Layer Cake Mountain in Kelowna are examples of volcanic action. Extinct volcanoes include Giant's Head near Summerland, Dilworth in Kelowna and Munson next to Penticton.

Then it got colder and ice came down from the north and put out the fires and sat on top of the Okanagan, which at that time didn't have a name, because there was no one to name it. The Okanagan Lobe of the Cordilleran ice sheet was more than a kilometre (.62 mile) thick. That made it heavy. The weight of it, along with movement and the coming and going of various other glaciers and their melting and leaving deposits, plus some land shifting, are responsible for the shape of the Valley.

Imagine a lake 100 metres (390 feet) up in the sky above the present lake. Imagine a glacial dam near Okanagan Falls, holding back the water. Imagine deposits of silt, sand, rocks and organic matter dropping to the bottom of that lake over thousands of years. Can't imagine that? Too bad, because no one took pictures. But if you need proof, look at the light-coloured bluffs just north of Penticton beside Highway 97. These are white silt bluffs, although locals prefer the alliteration of the name "clay cliffs." Look closely and you can see fine layers of sediment from silt falling to the bottom of the glacial lake. This was caused by heavy glaciers grinding over rocks and pulverizing them into flour.

After the climate settled down, some people hiked across a toll-free causeway that connected what we now call Asia and Alaska. This was, give or take a few millennia, quite a long time ago. It took 20,000 years before some of these travellers found retirement heaven in the Okanagan. They lived quite happily here and were mistakenly called "Indians" by those who came later. About 12,000 of them settled in the Okanagan. They developed a language known as Interior Salish and called the place they lived something like Oakinachen. These people, who may have called themselves Skiluxw, were hunters and collectors who lived off the land and had no need of agriculture.

European invaders were quite late in coming to the Okanagan, and, compared to other parts of the continent, they got along with the existing inhabitants reasonably well. Unfortunately, they introduced smallpox and influenza, which, literally, decimated the Native population.

David Stuart is thought to be the first outsider (outside of the first Native, who was also, at one time, an outsider) to see the Okanagan, back in 1811. He was scouting for the Pacific Fur Company and spent six and a half months on a ship coming from New York City to the Columbia River. At the point where the Okanagan River enters the Columbia he established a post. He and fellow explorer Ovid Montigny followed the Okanagan River north, met a Native chief on the way and traded him printed cloth and other material for four horses. Both parties thought they got a good deal.

Stuart did not think the Okanagan was much of a place in terms of furry animals so he kept going to the Thompson River, where the She-waps (later Shuswaps) were also easy to get along with and the beaver were so thick you could walk across rivers on their backs. After 188 days he returned to his original post with 2,500 beaver skins. Others followed his trail up the west side of Okanagan Lake and it became known as the Okanagan Fur Brigade Trail.

The first whites to settle down were missionaries: Oblates of Mary Immaculate. These Roman Catholics deprived themselves of fun and believed they should convert the poor to their version of God. Oblate, as well as meaning spherical, also means devoted in Latin. Fathers Charles Pandosy and Pierre Richard were among the first group to arrive in the autumn of 1859 to set up a mission. They knew a good thing when they saw it. Both kept getting transferred to other parts of the continent and Pandosy even went to France, but, like the modern tourist, he came back four times and finally semi-retired and died here in 1891. His mission, next to Mission Creek, is preserved on Benvoulin Rd. in Kelowna (see Kelowna, page 47).

Close to the time Father Pandosy was setting up in Kelowna, Hiram "Okanogan" Smith was building a trading post on the east side of Osoyoos Lake near Oroville, Washington, and he, like Father Pandosy, started growing fruit with a 1,200-tree apple orchard. The dates given for his settlement vary from 1857 to 1865 so it is difficult to say who was first (see Oroville, page 89).

Over a span of 32 years, a chapel, homes and other buildings were constructed under the direction of Father Pandosy. The Native people were willing trading partners, listened dutifully to the sermons and a few even became Catholics. That mission was the start of the wave of white settlement in the area and now there are close to 300,000 non-Natives living in the Okanagan.

The recorded history of this valley is amazingly short and it is one of the rare places on Earth where, outside of some minor skirmishes, there have been no wars, no rebellions, no uprisings and no armed insurrections.

There are only a few cabins, barns and farmhouses preserved from the years before 1890. Since that time it's a rather ordinary story about the quest for gold, for farmland, for range and for

Reaching for nearer the top

Where do Okanagan cities rank in the national scheme of populations? Websites put Kelowna at number 25 in Canada with a population of 136,600 — just 100 more souls than Abbotsford and 5,000 fewer than Trois-Rivières. If Vernon, Kelowna and Penticton were amalgamated the way Ottawa and Hull merge and Niagara and St. Catharines combine numbers, it could hop past Saskatoon and Regina (numbers 17 and 18), surpass Oshawa, leap Windsor and challenge Victoria (which claims Saanich) for a spot in the top 15 most populous urban areas.

timber, with many interesting anecdotes tossed in. Those who want more information will enjoy the assortment of historical sites, historical walks and museums that are described elsewhere in this book (see Books, page 159). The history lesson is over: let's get on with it.

BEST OF THE BEACHES

Fortunately, since Okanagan summers are long and hot, aquatic relief is always nearby and rarely is a beach or cove more than 10 minutes from any Okanagan location. There is shoreline for every specialized interest.

- For the warmest water head south to Osoyoos.
- If long stretches of sand are a waterfront requirement, Penticton is the place to be.
- If sunbathing and swimming *au naturel* is your cup of tea, then bare it in Kelowna.
- If you want secure swimming, Peachland provides the Valley's only lifeguards.
- If you desire secluded coves and a natural setting, then Kalamalka Lake is a great dive.

Warmest Waters

Osoyoos Lake vies with Christina Lake, 100 kilometres (62 miles) to the east, as the warmest body of water in Canada. Residents of both areas make that claim and both state that the summertime temperature of the water is the highest in the country. The summer temperature of the water in either lake is about 24°C (75°F).

I have done the breaststroke in Christina Lake in mid-September and found it quite comfortable and I've snorkelled at Osoyoos in early October and found it cool, but bearable. Try them both. In fact take a swim in January. Polar Bear dips are held in Kelowna and Peachland. Okanagan Lake does not freeze over, nor does Osoyoos Lake.

Once Okanagan Lake gets heated up, its waters stay warm until autumn. Since snow melting from the surrounding mountains feeds the lake, you can forget about taking a dip much before the end of May unless you find a shallow cove that the sun has been shining on for a week.

Sandy Shorelines

Skaha Lake provides long stretches of sand at both its south shore in Okanagan Falls and its north shore in Penticton. The south portion of Okanagan Lake, which is at the north end of Penticton, is also festooned with stretches of sand. That means you will find long

Hot Sands Beach at Kelowna's City Park

sandy beaches at either end of Penticton. These stretches total 3 kilometres (2 miles) in length and they are less than 5 kilometres (3 miles) apart.

Hot Sands beach in City Park in Kelowna lives up to its name in midsummer. Sandals are smart.

Naturally Nude

The nudists' natural shoreline is hidden from public view in Kelowna and is not that easy to find, but it is opposite St. Hubertus Estate Winery, on Lakeshore Rd., and is called Cedar Creek Park. Trails lead down to the nudist beach from the parking lot above.

On my "professional" visit to the nudist beach, on a hot sunny afternoon in early September, the majority of the bathers and sun worshippers were male couples. Scattered among them were a few female couples and just one opposite sex pairing. I'm told that's a normal mix.

Lifeguards

On Peachland's waterfront, lifeguards are on duty from 10 a.m. to 5 p.m. during the summer, and it is the only public beach where such security is offered. Most of the sandy beaches are safe with gradual drop-offs. The water depth beyond rocky shorelines is always unpredictable.

Whose Beach is it Anyway?

Shoreline access is an issue in the Okanagan, with the owners of huge lakeshore homes building walls, docks and fences into the water to keep the public away. There is considerable debate about where private land ends and public begins, but basically anyone walking in the water or on land that is within a metre or two (3 to 6 feet) of the water is likely to be on public land.

The dividing line between private and public is called the "natural boundary" and is defined as the visible high-water mark. This is the point where the action of the water is so common and usual as to leave a mark on the soil of the shore with a character distinct from the rest of the land. This could be a change in vegetation or the nature of the soil. With few exceptions (leases, marinas, etc.) land below this mark is crown land and the public has rights of access. In the many instances where landowners and their neighbours have dumped fill, landscaped or excavated, the high-water mark has vanished and guesswork is required. When the lake level is low, as it has been in recent years, the amount of public land that is not under water increases. Docks require a government license that costs $650 for 10 years.

Secluded Coves

Several secluded coves can be found at Paul's Tomb in Kelowna. Go to the very north end of Ellis St. and take the road up Knox Mountain to the first lookout on the left. Park if you are driving (it's a steep but enjoyable bike ride or hike) and then take the gravel footpath downhill to the shoreline and go right for a couple of kilometres (a bit more than a mile). Remember, you have to come back up again.

An alternative route to Paul's Tomb is to turn left at the stop sign at the end of Ellis onto Poplar Point Dr., which follows the lakeshore. Follow it up the hill and turn left when it stops. At a metal barrier on the right, start walking or biking along the trail until you come to some portable toilets, then follow the path to the coves. Parking can be a problem on weekends as there is only room for a half-dozen cars. Either way, the trail is less than 3 kilometres (2 miles) to a delightful, rocky swimming spot that seems to be in the middle of the wilderness.

Paul's Tomb is the burial place of Rembler Paul and his wife. They owned a large cottage on the lakeshore and excavated a spacious tomb, suitable for six, in the rocky cliff above the lake. Mrs. Paul died first and he followed, at age 85, in 1916. They were the only ones to be entombed. The actual tomb, made of cement up to 40 centimetres (16 inches) thick, with a steel door, is not easy to find. It is about 30 metres (100 feet) in elevation above the lake and 100 metres (330 feet) from the shore. A worn foot trail leads to it. The steel door is about all that can be seen.

OKANAGAN WEATHER

In a phrase: temperate, with long dry summers and moderate winters. It's the prime reason people live and retire here. The Okanagan gets more than 2,000 hours of sun per year, with the vast majority coming in the summer. From Armstrong south to Osoyoos the weather goes from colder to hotter, and wetter to dryer. The differential is usually about 10 percent.

The rain shadow effect of the Coast Mountains is most strongly felt in the southwestern portions of the Valley, with increasing precipitation to the north and east.

American visitors might find the metric system somewhat confusing although most Canadians are bi-thermal, bi-dimensional and bi-lingual. The United States is pretty much alone in using its odd measuring system and sooner or later (probably later) it will fall in line with the rest of the world. Until then, the chart on the following page will help southern visitors make sense of Canadian temperatures.

Dry Spell

The summer of 2003 was the driest on record in the Valley. How dry? No significant precipitation fell between June 1 and September 8. During that time brief showers in the central Okanagan totalled just 23 millimetres (one inch) of precipitation. The dry spell included 44 straight days of constant sun and no precipitation. A trace of rain fell at the beginning of September and another six dry days followed before a significant downpour on September 8.

Nearly every day topped 30°C with full sunshine. With low humidity, that's vacation weather! In fact, relative humidity drops from mean winter values of 80 percent to 50 percent in summer.

Don't expect to be refreshed by a summer breeze in Kelowna. It has the calmest air in Canada with the greatest percentage of wind observations per year of calm conditions (39 percent). On the other hand, the wind chill factor isn't a factor in winter. Penticton and other Okanagan cities have considerably more wind.

Fahrenheit/Celsius Conversions

FAHRENHEIT	CELSIUS
122°	50°
104°	40°
86°	30°
68°	20°
50°	10°
32°	0°
14°	−10°
−4°	−20°
−22°	−30°

Most Desirable Climate

In a survey by Environment Canada, the Okanagan received top honours for having "the most desirable climate in Canada." Through the application of the Climate Severity Index, based on such factors as discomfort, hazard, outdoor mobility and the psychological effects associated with them, Environment Canada confirmed what Okanagan residents already know — the Valley is truly a one-of-a-kind region and, as Environment Canada stated, the climate is conducive to less stress.

Frost-Free Growing

This key gardening statistic varies immensely from year to year, from north to south and, above all, from low elevations to high. The shortest frost-free stretch (safe for tomato plants) in recent records is 90 days in Vernon, while the longest is 226 days in Osoyoos with temperatures, both day and night, remaining above freezing. Here are some average figures for frost-free days, from north to south. Elevation, and location of the reporting stations, may account for some variations.

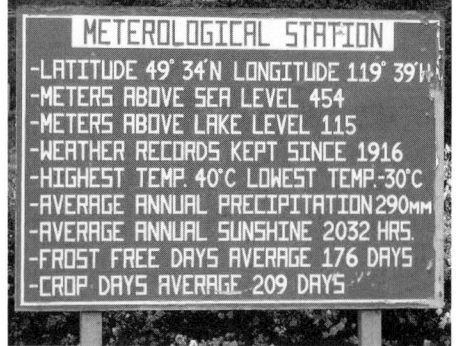

Weather at Summerland Ornamental Gardens

Salmon Arm	149 days	Penticton	142 days
Vernon	145 days	Oliver	141 days
Kelowna	140 days	Osoyoos	182 days
Summerland	175 days		

Central Okanagan Temperatures (in Celsius)

MONTH	DAILY MAX.	DAILY MIN.	MEAN	EXTREME MAX.	EXTREME MIN.
January	0.0	−6.5	−3.3	12.2	−31.1
February	4.0	−4.1	−0.1	17.2	−28.3
March	8.0	−1.8	3.3	21.1	−22.2
April	14.5	2.0	8.3	27.8	−9.4
May	20.1	6.5	13.3	33.9	−3.9
June	23.9	10.5	17.2	35.6	−1.1
July	27.9	12.9	20.4	38.9	3.3
August	26.8	12.1	19.5	36.1	0.6
September	21.1	7.6	14.3	33.9	−5.6
October	13.6	2.6	8.1	25.6	−10.0
November	6.3	−1.1	2.6	18.3	−22.8
December	2.3	−3.7	−0.7	14.4	−24.4

OKANAGAN FRUIT GROWING

To Father Pandosy, whose mission was to spread the word of God to the Native community, and to "Okanogan" Smith, who was in the trading post business in Washington, the adaptability of the local climate for fruit growing was immediately obvious. Pandosy started the wine industry with his plantings of grapevines for sacramental wine. At the same time, in the 1850s, Smith imported seedlings for the first apple orchard. Their groundwork is obvious to anyone who sets foot in the Valley. One could make a good case for declaring agriculture to be the most important activity in the Okanagan.

The following chart shows the fruit-growing seasons for central Okanagan. Osoyoos can be two weeks earlier, Penticton one week earlier and Vernon a week later.

FRUIT	BLOSSOM	HARVEST
Apples	May 5 – May 20	August 15 – October 30
Apricots	April 10 – April 25	July 20 – August 10
Cherries	April 20 – May 7	Mid June – August 1
Grapes	April 25 – May 20	September 5 – October 10
Peaches	April 20 – May 2	July 25 – September 1
Pears	April 25 – May 10	August 15 – September 30
Prunes/Plums	April 28 – May 10	August 15 – September 10

New Bites on the Block

The Ambrosia apple is the current darling of the orchardists—60,000 boxes are picked each year. While this is a small portion of the 165 million pounds (75 million kilograms) of apples grown here, production of this tasty apple has recently doubled. The excitement is about an apple that was discovered on a tree in a Similkameen orchard in a row previously planted in Red and Delicious trees but recently replanted to Jonagold. The unexplained offspring is superior in taste, texture and colour to its parents. This three-colour apple is now planted throughout the Valley and supplants many of the standard varieties. It is a late-September harvest and stays fresh for eating and baking.

A new red fruit is brightening the cherry orchards after the usual crop has been harvested in June and July. The late harvest Staccato cherry, which ripens in late August, will give the Okanagan the only cherry harvest in the world at that date. The research station in Summerland is also working on a cherry that ripens in September. As shipping and refrigeration have improved over the decades, the market for fresh cherries has dominated. At one time there were a dozen canneries in the Okanagan but they have vanished.

Darling Starling

In 1983 a flock of 25,000 starlings was reported in Oliver. If a gathering even one-tenth that size descends on an orchard the owner could lose 20 percent of a cherry crop in a few hours. The birds, introduced to North America from Europe in the late 1800s, love cherries and also enjoy pecking indiscriminately at apples—ruining them for the market with a single poke. The starlings have abandoned being snowbirds and now the majority stay home for the winter.

The cacophonous explosions that rock much of rural Okanagan in the summer months are propane-powered cannons. The noise is designed to scare the birds from trees and vines. Netting can also be used and various types of fluttering ribbons act as a deterrent. As a final resource, the Okanagan has a starling stalker. He captures the birds in traps and then puts them permanently to sleep with a dose of carbon monoxide or chloroform.

How Much Fruit?

The value of the fruit that goes through the four packinghouses in the Okanagan is about $100 million.

IT CONSISTS OF:

Apples	4.3 million 40-pound boxes
Pears	250,000 45-pound boxes
Peaches	180,000 20-pound cartons
Cherries	170,000 20-pound cartons
Plums	25,000 20-pound cartons
Apricots	22,000 20-pound cartons
Nectarines	20,000 20-pound cartons

The most popular apples, in order, are Red Delicious, MacIntosh, Gala, Spartan, Golden, Fuji, Jonagold, Granny Smith and Braeburn.

Cantaloupe Capital

Oliver was once known as the Cantaloupe Capital of Canada but now focusses on wine. Besides cantaloupes you can buy, at many roadside stands, watermelons, strawberries, raspberries, tomatoes, cherries, apricots, peaches, plums, apples, pears, grapes, peppers, asparagus, cucumbers, peas, squash, corn and walnuts. That's in addition to various currants, gourds, herbs, flowers ... a full list tests both memory and imagination.

OKANAGAN LITE:
Delicious Spartan Meets Granny Smith's Empire

Technical Data: Angle of the Sun

At 50 degrees north latitude (Kelowna) the angle of the sun at winter solstice is 16 degrees above the horizon and on June 22 it is 63 degrees. At the U.S. border it is 1.5 degrees higher.

On the teacher's desk, keeping the doctor away, luring Eve — it's the apple, an outstanding icon of appreciation, good health and temptation.

Kids don't plunk a grapefruit on the teacher's desk if they have aspirations of being the class pet; a pumpkin a day doesn't keep the doctor away, and, if it had been a pear, papaya or pomegranate in the garden of Eden, you can bet Eve wouldn't have given it a sideways glance.

When it comes to target practice what are you going to put on your son's head to split with an arrow? An olive, raspberry or stalk of rhubarb? No, a big beautiful Spartan or a shiny Granny Smith.

And who is the master of fecundity that roams a barren landscape — Johnny Bananaseed? Johnny Tamarind Seed?

Did I mention what caused Sir Isaac Newton to develop his theory of gravitational pull? If he had been sitting under a coconut palm he might have discovered something more mundane, like a theory of concussion.

If I was stranded on a desert island and could have only one item to eat (pizza doesn't count as one) it would be an apple. You can not only slice 'em an' dice 'em but they bake, roast, juice, fill a pig's mouth, turn to sauce, work as a puck for road hockey, serve as a home for a pet worm and provide amusement by trying to create a peel equal to your height. I could lose my drool thinking about apple dumplings, apple pies, applesauce, dried apple, apple cider, apple butter, Snapple, mock apple ... the appellations are endless.

Compared to the monotony of flavours from other fruit, apples range from a tongue-twisting tart that sucks your cheeks together, to soft and mellow.

Lesser fruit tends to come in one basic colour, but the apple drops from the tree in delicious reds, granny greens, russet browns and ambrosic yellows. Transparents are almost white. Mother Nature will even put a logo on an apple with some astute blocking of the sun. Try that with a blueberry.

At Halloween, bobbing for fruit in a water-filled tub is a tradition. And what fruit is worth getting wet for on a cold October night? Not the date, the ugli or the kumquat. No, a kid would only risk drowning for an apple.

One of the joys of an Okanagan winter is wandering through the B.C. Fruit Packers' Co-operative on Clement Ave. in Kelowna, where the aroma of just-sliced apples fills the cool crisp air. The big Mutsus and Fujis are my favourites and I wait impatiently for the Jonagold's brief appearance. Practically next-door is the Sun-Rype factory, where dried apple provides a leathery snack both nutritious and delicious. On the warehouse floor are thousands of cartons of apple juice blends and mixes with orange, peach and pineapple.

LIFE IN THE OKANAGAN

Close to 300,000 people make their homes in the Okanagan. Statistically it is difficult to find figures that show they are significantly different from other Canadians. They don't earn a great deal more, they are not employed in greater numbers, the crime rate is neither high nor low and they don't connect to the Internet with any more or less frequency than the typical Canadian.

Something that the visitor would not notice, unless time was spent questioning locals, is that very few Okanagan residents were actually born here. Many are seniors who have farmed or engaged in other occupations on the prairies and spent their summer vacations on the shores of Okanagan Lake. When retirement time rolled around, they made the decision to make their vacation land their home. Others left big cities like Vancouver, Edmonton and Calgary for the improved climate and a quieter, less pressured lifestyle. Following are some facts that illustrate the benefits of living in the Okanagan.

Live Long, Be Prosperous

Want to live longer? Then the Okanagan is the place to be.

You'll gain an extra two years of life on planet Earth if you make your home in this sunny interior valley. Canadians, on average, live 78.3 years. Statistics Canada gives the average life span of an Okanagan resident as 80.3 years.

The average income for the 59,610 residents who have reached age 65 is $21,900 in Penticton and Vernon, and $2,000 more than that in Kelowna.

The local health authority credits the beauty of the rugged terrain for encouraging physical fitness. The percentage of obese people in the Okanagan is lower than the Canadian average, which is 13 percent.

Language Stays Stable

While the language structure of Canada diversifies, the languages spoken in the Okanagan, specifically Kelowna, are hardly changing at all.

English is the mother tongue of 84.9 percent of the Kelowna population according to Statistics Canada, virtually unchanged from 1996. Nationally 59.7 percent cite English as their mother tongue and 23.1 percent claim French. Figures from the 2001 census show that in the rest of Canada the number of people speaking a language other than the two official languages grew by 12.5 percent but in Kelowna there was a slight decline.

The next most popular language, German, decreased by .67 percent. French, the third most popular mother tongue,

Go South, Get Old

The farther south one travels in the Okanagan the older the population gets.

PERCENTAGE OF POPULATION AGE 65 AND OLDER:

	2001	2031 EST.
North Okanagan	17	25
South Okanagan	24	31
B.C. Average	13	23

increased by a minuscule .04 percent while the next two, Ukrainian and Punjabi, went down slightly. The number of native Italian speakers increased a little and the number of Dutch speakers went up from 515 to 640.

WHAT CAME FIRST? THE OGOPOGO OR THE EGG?

Deep, dark Okanagan Lake is home to Ogopogo, a leviathan that rivals Scotland's Loch Ness monster in elusiveness and fame. There are statues of a friendly Ogopogo on the downtown lakeshore in Kelowna and in Polson Park in Vernon.

Before the white man arrived, N'ha-a-itk, the lake monster, lived in a cave near Squally Point, opposite Peachland. Any Native who paddled near the lair of N'ha-a-itk kept a small animal in the canoe to be thrown overboard as a sacrifice to appease the serpent, for often a storm would mysteriously spring up and the demon would take a life.

Sightings of Ogopogo usually number about seven per year according to local writer Arlene Gaal, who has penned two volumes about the mysterious lake monster. She says Okanagan Mountain Park has been a favoured sighting spot in recent years and, not surprisingly, most sightings come between March and October. That's more a reflection of when people are out and looking rather than when the sea serpent seeks the surface. Hikers in the park have, on occasion, spotted "something quite large in the water and were able to make out a fair amount of detail," says Gaal. "Right down to the whiskers on its face."

In addition to Gaal's books, several documentaries have been made for television, boats have scanned the lake with sonar, a CD has been recorded in Germany and hundreds of blurry pictures have been taken.

In 1990 and 1991 a Japanese TV film crew came to get pictures of the Peachland Pet, but even with cameras in submersibles they came away without a definitive fin on film.

F. M. Buckland of Kelowna told this story about several people camping near the lake in 1914,

> "One of the party ... was attracted by a strong smell of rotted fish ... and found the badly decomposed body of a strange animal lying at the water's edge. The body was between five and six feet in length, and would weigh about 400 pounds. It had a short, broad, flat tail, and a head that stuck out between shoulders without any sign of neck, the nose was stubby, and sticking out of a rounded head, and no ears visible. The hide was sparsely covered with silky hair, four or five inches in length and of a bluish grey colour, while the teeth resembled those of a great bird...."

For years, a shoulder blade, the ivory-like tusks and great claws were shown to interested people, but now this evidence has disappeared.

How Ogopogo Got His/Her Name

According to a report of the Okanagan Historical Society: "After World War One, there was in Vernon an organization of amateurs who, under the title of The Kalamalka Players, gave many entertainments, and raised thousands of dollars for charitable projects. In one of the performances, Mr. Brimblecombe sang *The Ogopogo Song*, which, after World War 1, had captivated England. H. F. Beattie wrote a parody of the popular song.

The chorus of the original started:

I'm looking for the Ogopogo. The funny little Ogopogo.
His mother was an earwig, his father was a snail.

The chorus of the parody:

I'm looking for the Ogopogo
The bunny-hugging Ogopogo
His mother was a mutton and his father was a whale
I'm going to put a little bit of salt on his tail.

Kelowna's Ogopogo statue

OKANAGAN LiTE:
Ogopogo Woe — 10 years and nothing to show

Ogopogo's press agent has stirred up a storm of publicity: movies, scientific research and a big reward for bringing in the lake leviathan dead or alive — either on the end of a harpoon or flopping in a net.

The thing that hasn't stirred is the monster itself.

If he/she doesn't soon rear his/her scaly head the whole lake monster thing will become a dead issue and Ogie will be presumed to be dead tissue.

A lot is riding on a resurgence of Peachland's prehistoric pet. Manufacturers of everything from yoghurt to fertilizer depend on the viability of the legend to lend credence to their Ogopogo logos.

I heard from an occasionally reliable source that a Lake Monster Hall of Fame is planned for Peachland. This attraction must compete for tourist dollars against the house made out of embalming fluid bottles near Creston, so it has to be good. Another year of a no-show Ogopogo will scuttle the plans, which include a wax replica of Nessie, a web-footed Yeti and an abominable sturgeon.

The promoter claims that UFOs (Unidentified Floating Objects) on the lake are Ogopogo scat. The bathroom habits of a 20-ton mammoth are nothing to sneer at, especially by water skiers who, in fact, could pound into a mound of Ogopogo poo at 50 kilometres per hour (31 mph).

Some fresh Ogopogo sightings would generate a scuba diving industry, glass-bottom boat tours for ogre and ogie oglers and the manufacture of all sorts of rubber lake monsters for kids. Bouncing green Ogopogo sticks would be a natural, as would glass souvenirs that, when inverted, send down a shower of pogonip (that's an icy fog). The head honcho of a local dojo is going with an Ogopogo judo logo.

Unfortunately we don't have a ripple of excitement. Not even a pogonophoran — a wormlike marine animal. The sightings we do get are pathetic: alcohol-induced, 2 a.m. glimpses of big things with fins submerging just before the cameras, or anything else, are focussed.

Action is needed. A few freshwater sharks imported from Nicaragua would be a good start. A 30-kilogram (50-pound) sturgeon from Russia would help.

The Ogopogo legend is not likely to reach fruition until either the monster surfaces (Hell may become a land of igloos first) or a foreign conglomerate gobbles him up and packages him like a talking mouse with big ears.

Until then somebody needs to give the palindromic Ogopogo a poke.

Vernon's Ogopogo statue

Boardwalk along Kelowna's
lakeshore

2 CiTiES AND SETTLEMENTS

THE OKANAGAN VALLEY | POPULATION: 297,600

More than 200 arts, heritage and agri-tourism attractions in the Okanagan have been identified. The inventory includes 42 wineries, 28 other agri-tourism attractions, 17 museums, 14 heritage attractions, 19 art galleries, 12 performing arts groups, 15 cultural festivals and 45 artists' studios.

In the central Okanagan, arts and culture account for 2,368 full- and part-time jobs. The cultural economy is responsible for 3.8 percent of regional employment.

The new Okanagan office of the B.C. Restaurant and Foodservices Association has 200 members, but says, "The estimated number of restaurants in the Valley could be 1,000 if you count coffee shops, golf courses, wineries and ski hill eateries as well as casual restaurants and fine dining rooms."

The city descriptions that follow are listed from north to south within three areas: the Okanagan, B.C., the Okanogan, Washington and North of the Okanagan.

ARMSTRONG | POPULATION: 4,200
The Okanagan Starts Here

Just north of Armstrong, at a rundown picnic stop beside Highway 97, a sign declares that this spot is the "Okanagan Great Divide." South of the sign all surface water flows south into the Columbia River and then into the Pacific Ocean at the Washington/Oregon State border. North of the sign the water flows to the Thompson and Fraser rivers and into the ocean at Vancouver. Technically it's not a "Great" divide and confusing the issue is Fortune Creek, which flows north, from south of the sign, and goes under Highway 97.

Former Armstrong resident Sheila Jenks explains it this way: "It is confusing, especially since Fortune Creek and Deep Creek are at one point less than a kilometre from one another. Fortune Creek flows from the northwest side of Silver Star area, and it comes down to Armstrong... right at this point is the Divide, which causes it to flow north to Enderby, then join the Shuswap River system, north through Mara Lake and eventually into the Shuswap lakes, then west to the Thompson-Fraser system. Deep Creek flows the opposite way — south through Armstrong to Otter Lake and into Okanagan Lake, then through the Okanagan to eventually join the Columbia River basin system."

First named Aberdeen by the early settlers and sometimes referred to as Celery City, the official name came from W. C. Heaton-Armstrong, who floated the bonds to bring the railway to the town and got his eponymous reward.

When work was completed on the Shuswap/Okanagan Railway in 1892, the settlement of Armstrong consisted of a lone boxcar that served as railway station and home for the rail agent. Lansdowne, the largest settlement in surrounding Spallumcheen, had been bypassed by the rail line, so the citizens of that community picked up their buildings and quickly resettled beside the tracks in Armstrong. Armstrong is in the midst of the Spallumcheen Valley and the railway, flanked by flower beds, trees and stone walls, still bisects the centre of the old-fashioned western town. Trains rumble through twice a day and during the night. At harvest time lighted pumpkins are lined up along the walls beside the tracks. The town hopes to set a record for the most pumpkins on a wall — several thousand. The pumpkins are put up after the Harvest Pumpkin Festival in early October.

Armstrong Memorial to Catherine O'Hare Schubert

The big building in the centre of town, on the south side of the tracks, is the Armstrong Hotel, first built in 1892. It immediately burned to the ground, and then was quickly rebuilt the next year.

Other Attractions

All Okanagan phone numbers are in the 250 area.

Armstrong/Spallumcheen Museum and Art Gallery
Pleasant Valley Rd., 546-8318, www.armstrongbc.com/museumandartgallery. The museum features the history of the area and the art gallery displays the work of local artists.

Caravan Farm Theatre
R.R. 4, Old Kamloops Highway, 546-8533, 1-866-546-8533, www.caravanfarmtheatre.com.

This 32-hectare (80-acre) farm produces both organic vegetables and plays. Theatrical works range from Shakespeare to new, original works created especially for the Farm. Music, mask, puppetry, song, dance and outdoor staging are often combined. Workshops in aspects of theatre as well as farming are offered. In winter a horse-drawn sleigh ride, which includes a performance,

The Lady Overlander

One of the most interesting and courageous citizens, not only of Armstrong, but also of North America, is Catherine O'Hare Schubert, the first woman to come overland to British Columbia.

Born in Ireland in 1835, she sailed to United States at age 16 and worked as a maid. In her spare time she taught herself to read.

At 19 she married a 27-year-old German carpenter, Augustus Schubert, and they moved west to St. Paul, Minnesota. Catherine opened a grocery store and baked bread while Augustus did carpentry. Their first two

CONTINUES ON PAGE 37

is a major attraction. The Farm has an organic vegetable garden and a Clydesdale horse-breeding program.

Chickadee Ridge Miniatures
1403 McLeod Rd., 546-9323.

Just north of town near the "Okanagan Great Divide" sign. The main attraction is miniature horses, but there are also little donkeys, goats, sheep, cows and bunnies and various birds, from tiny quail and doves to huge emus, pheasants, peacocks and wild turkeys. Chickadee Ridge describes itself as "the largest miniature horse-breeding farm in Canada."

Farmers' Market
Held seasonally at the Exhibition grounds in Armstrong on Saturdays, 8 a.m. to noon.

Drive-In Theatre
933 Highway 97, 838-6757, www.telus.net/starlight. (between Enderby and Armstrong)

The Starlight Drive-In rates mention for both nostalgia and novelty. Before drive-in banking and fast foods the term meant just one thing — a place where you sat in your car and watched movies on a distant screen while sound crackled from a metal box hung from your car window. Families bundled up the kids, and young couples went with the intention of not spending a lot of time watching the movie. There are very few drive-ins left in North America but one of them, just south of Enderby, is the Starlight. In summer the show doesn't start until nearly 10 p.m. and the double feature isn't likely to end before 2 a.m.

The Armstrong Fair
At the beginning of September, is the largest agricultural fair in B.C. (See Festivals and Events, Interior Provincial Exhibition.)

Armstrong Dining
The scope is somewhat limited — moderately priced, home-style restaurants are the predominant Armstrong fare. Walk the main street and they are not hard to spot.

The Brown Derby
2510 Pleasant Valley Blvd., 546–8221,

The Brown Derby is in a house once owned by a child of Catherine Schubert. The decor is simple, prices reasonable and the owners will happily give directions or exchange witticisms. Voted "best breakfast" in the North Okanagan. The tourist information centre also recommends The Pea Pod.

Armstrong Wine

Hunting Hawk Winery
4758 Gulch Rd., 546–2164.

children were born, and when a depression hit the area, the family packed up and moved north to Winnipeg (then Fort Garry). In the spring of 1862 a group of 150 men arrived. They were following the "overland" route to the Cariboo to find gold. Augustus decided to join these Overlanders and get his share of the yellow wealth. Rather than stay behind (as other women did) and operate the farm and the store and raise her children, Catherine elected to accompany her husband and became the only woman among more than 150 men heading west.

She was pregnant with child number four (the others were aged five, three and one) when they set off on the arduous trek. They made it to British Columbia and were travelling down the Thompson River on a raft when Catherine went into labour. They went ashore at a Native village where the women helped to deliver a healthy girl that she named Rose. The search for gold was a failure and in 1881 Augustus gave up prospecting and they bought a farm in the Okanagan. When he died in 1908 Catherine moved to Armstrong, where she became an important part of the community. She died 10 years later, and a monument to her courage stands in the town's park. Several streets carry the name Schubert. The full story of her trip with the Overlanders remains to be told. Rose Swanson Mountain was named after Catherine Schubert's fourth child.

The Big Cheese

Armstrong has been known for its production of cheese for close to a century. The Armstrong Cheese Co-operative operated from 1902 to 1961 and at one point was the second-largest cheese producer in Canada.
The Armstrong brand of cheese is now made in several Canadian factories by Montreal-based Saputo Foods and is brought to Armstrong from Abbotsford. The closure of the big cheese factory at 3155 Pleasant Valley Rd., which was recently used for bottling milk, was announced in September 2003.

VILLAGE CHEESE COMPANY, (3475 Smith Dr., 1-888-633-8899, www.villagecheese.com) carries on the tradition of making cheese in Armstrong. It's under the clock in the new part of town close to the highway. Here visitors can watch cheese being made in stainless steel vats and they can sample chocolate cheese, blueberry cheese, goats' milk cheese, beer cheese and other interesting flavours. This is the home of Farmstead Artisan Cheese, which has won numerous awards.

SPALLUMCHEEN | POPULATION: 5,535

By area, Spallumcheen, 17 kilometres (10 miles) northeast of Vernon, is the largest district municipality in B.C. The name comes from Interior Salish for "beautiful place" or "beautiful valley." The first community, Lansdowne, was abandoned when the railway bypassed it in favour of flatter Armstrong in 1892. All that remains is the cemetery. Armstrong incorporated as a separate city in 1913, creating the strange situation of one municipality — Armstrong — surrounded by another, Spallumcheen. Agriculture has always been the primary industry, cloaking local hills in rich green alfalfa and golden grains.

VERNON | POPULATION: 36,500

Named after Forbes George Vernon, chief commissioner of Lands and Works for British Columbia. The luxuriant growth of bunchgrass in the Valley attracted cattle ranchers to the region in the 1860s and 1870s.

There are a few places to sample the early Vernon vegetation and early Vernon settlement. One is Kalamalka Provincial Park, where the grasslands are preserved and you can get a feeling for the terrain of this part of the Valley before development. Another is the restored O'Keefe Ranch, founded in 1867 by Cornelius O'Keefe. At that time, huge cattle ranches occupied the Valley, and ranch headquarters were self-contained settlements. By the turn of the century O'Keefe and his partner owned 8,090 hectares (20,000 acres) of prime land.

One of the first things a visitor to Vernon notices is that the city has been painted — and not in plain pastels or institutional greens, but colourful, dynamic murals. Everywhere you look in Vernon you come face to face with larger-than-life characters. Close to 30 huge paintings depict the shaping of the community and more murals are added each year. Two of the featured artists, Michelle Loughery and Sarah Lindsay, have also done murals in New York City. Downtown wall-art is somewhat trendy these days, but the big pictures turn bare brick and crass concrete into an interesting cityscape. A brochure outlining a two-kilometre (a bit more than a mile) walking tour of the art can be obtained at city hall, many stores or the tourist information centres.

Vernon shares with Kelowna and Vancouver the honour of having the best downtown parks in British Columbia. Polson Park, at the junction of Highways 97 and 6, is a perfect spot for a picnic, a stroll or a game. It features tennis, lawn bowling, gardens, a water park, a play area for kids, sports fields, benches, tables, walking paths, a Japanese garden, a floral clock and a band shell. The Okanagan Science Centre and the Vernon Art Gallery are adjacent. Vernon Creek trickles through it.

Vernon is next to three lakes but, unlike the other major Okanagan communities, the main city isn't quite on any of them. Swan Lake to the north is a shallow bird sanctuary, but the other two have prime boating and bathing. To the west, an arm of Okanagan Lake features Kin Beach and Paddlewheel Park, while Kalamalka Lake, directly south, has summer amenities at Kal Beach.

Highway or Byway?
Vernon to Kelowna

From downtown Vernon take 34th St. south. It becomes Mission Rd. and then Commonage Rd. and passes the Allan Brooks Nature Centre on the left (great view of three lakes). It turns to hard-packed dirt and gravel as it slowly wanders through a quiet rural landscape known as "The Commonage" (a place to pasture in common). Stop at Rose's Lake, on the right, and see how many birds you can identify, particularly in the aspen grove. When the road ends at a T-junction you can turn left on Bailey Rd. and descend on pavement to Highway 97 and you are practically at Oyama. To continue on the byway route, turn right (still called Commonage Rd.) and pass the prestigious Predator Ridge golf course and surrounding developments. You pass a few pretty ponds and after 14 kilometres (8 miles) you are in Carr's Landing on Okanagan Lake. About 7 kilometres (4 miles) later you face a choice of going left on Okanagan Centre Rd. East or right on Okanagan Centre Rd. West. Since you are not on this route because you are in hurry, go right and follow the road as it meanders to Okanagan Centre, on the lake. About 40 kilometres (25 miles) after leaving Vernon, this road meets Glenmore Rd. A left turn and then a quick right will take you to Highway 97 in Winfield.

Turning right on Glenmore takes you to Kelowna where Glenmore changes its name to Spall just before it meets Highway 97 (Harvey Ave.).

Vernon Culture and Learning

Allan Brooks Nature Centre
250 Allan Brooks Way (follow 34th St. south), 260-4227, www.abnc.ca.

This former weather station has been turned into a centre that displays and explains the natural environment of the north Okanagan. The view from the Centre is one of the few easily accessible points where three lakes are in plain view: Swan, Okanagan and Kalamalka. Inside the building are science and nature displays geared to kids and school groups. Outside, a short trail wanders through the surrounding field with signs explaining the attempts to restore the original bunchgrass by eliminating the alien weeds. Allan Brooks came to the Okanagan in 1905 and was a leading North American bird illustrator. His pictures were featured in many magazines and galleries.

Davison Orchards

3111 Davison Rd., 549-3266, www.davison orchards.ca.

This family farm, on 20 hectares (50 acres) overlooking Vernon, has been selling homegrown fruit and vegetables, flowers, apple pies and fresh apple juice since 1933. It features heritage displays, farm animals, a picnic area, a children's play area and orchard tours. Go west on 30th Ave. from Vernon.

Gallery Vertigo

3001 31st St. (upstairs)

Eight artists have studios and there are two exhibition rooms, a reading lounge and a workshop.

Okanagan Science Centre

2704 Highway 6, 545-3644, www.okscience.ca.

Fun and education for kids, with two major exhibits—such as chemistry and electricity—that change every few months. Also camps for kids by the day or week, birthday parties and other special events.

O'Keefe Ranch

12 kilometres (8 miles) north of Vernon on Highway 97 in Spallumcheen Valley, 542-7868.

This prosperous cattle ranch was founded in 1867 by Cornelius O'Keefe and was operated by his family for the next 110 years. He made his first money as a cattle drover herding beef, purchased for $15 a head in Oregon, across the Columbia and Fraser rivers and across mountain ranges to the gold-mining communities in the Cariboo, where they fetched $150 apiece. O'Keefe and partner Thomas Greenhow pre-empted 129 hectares (320 acres) of land near the lake and started buying land on rivers and creeks for one dollar an acre from the government. Eventually they had 5,000 hectares (12,000 acres) on which they raised cattle, sheep, pigs and wheat. The ranch features tours of the restored O'Keefe home, an active blacksmith shop, saddle-making shop, church, general store, cookstove display, fowl pens, post office and museum with HO gauge model railway. The Ranch has a continuous calendar of special weekend activities such as horse shows, a cowboy festival, a motorcycle rally, a muscle car show and an antique farm equipment display.

O'Keefe Ranch

Planet Bee

5011 Bella Vista Rd., 542-8088, 1-877-233-9675, www. planetbee.com.

Sales of bee products (honey, beeswax, propolis, etc.) and a presentation: "world of the honeybee." Outdoor apiary and observation area. Next to Davison Orchards.

Vernon Museum and Archives

3009 32nd Ave., 542-3142, www.vernonmuseum.ca.

Artefacts demonstrate natural history, Native history and the growth and development of the region. A good source for information on walking and driving tours of the historic and heritage sites in the Vernon area. The museum also has a large collection of Kettle Valley Railway artefacts and memorabilia.

Vernon Art Gallery

3228 31st Ave., 545-3173.

Founded in 1945. More than 27,000 visitors per year view exhibits by local and guest artists.

Vernon Amusements

Atlantis Water Slides

7921 Highway 97, 549-4121.

Slides for all ages, a hot tub, mini golf, and volleyball. Five kilometres (3 miles) north of Vernon.

Boat Tour

545-8388, www.cruiseokanagan.com.

Cruises of Okanagan Lake, aboard the Spirit of the Okanagan, start from Paddlewheel Park.

Casino

Lake City Casinos, Village Green Hotel
4801 27th St., 545-3505,
www.lakecitycasinos.com.

Car Racing

Sun Valley Motor Speedway,
9531 Highway 97, 542-9090
www.sunvalleyspeedway.com.

The new facility features CASCAR, dwarf cars, pickups, IMCA modified, street stock and many other categories.

Cars roll towards the camera at Magnetic Hill

Magnetic Hill

At approximately 5300 Dixon Dam Rd., between Hughes Rd. and Hartnell Rd.

You may have heard about the magnetic hill in New Brunswick that appears to pull vehicles uphill. This one is better, but getting to it is tricky and there are no signs. From Highway 97 turn east onto 43rd Ave. At Pleasant Valley Rd. turn left. Two blocks later turn right on BX Rd. (also called 46th Ave.). It twists and turns and changes names constantly, next becoming East Vernon Rd. At the sign for Briggs Rd. go left. After the sharp turn the road becomes Dixon Dam Rd. Continue for less than a kilometre (.6 mile) and turn left at the sign for Dixon Dam Rd. (it continues ahead as Hartnell). Shortly you will see a group of dead trees (possibly alders) on the left. Stop your vehicle about halfway past this group of trees, put your car in neutral, and, amazingly, you will apparently start to coast backwards up the hill that you thought you were going down. Magnetic Hill B&B is just past the dead trees, on the left.

Polson Park

Paintball
Bushwacker Paintball Games, 5925 Hartnell Rd., Vernon, 542–1170, www.bushwackerpaintball.com.

Opal mining
Okanagan Opal Inc., 7879 Highway 97, 542–1103, www. opalscanada.com.

The showroom at the north end of Vernon displays many types of opals, including locally named Kalamalka crystal and Okanagan wildfire. Those who want to find their own opals can join a weekend convoy that goes to the mine, 40 kilometres (25 miles) west of Vernon at an elevation of 1,400 metres (4,500 feet).

Vernon Nature and Outdoors

Ellison Provincial Park,
On the east side of Okanagan Lake, a few kilometres (about a mile) south of Vernon, the park has walking trails with access to the head-lands that separate two beautiful bays that are good fishing spots. A car-top boat launch is located just north of the park, and a full boat-launch facility is 8 kilometres (5 miles) north. This is an area of undu-lating benchland dominated by stands of ponderosa pine and Douglas fir, set between the rolling hills of the Thompson Plateau to the west and the peaks of the Monashee Mountains to the east. Otter Bay, in the park, is the site of western Canada's first freshwater scuba diving and snorkelling park. A number of objects have been sunk here to attract a variety of fish and other lake-dwelling creatures.

Kalamalka Beach (Kal Beach)
On the north shore of Kalamalka Lake. The beach has volleyball courts, a long swimming pier and change and rest rooms. A conces-sion is open in the summer, as well as kayak and small boat rentals.

Kalamalka Lake Provincial Park

Eight kilometres (5 miles) south of Vernon off Kalamalka Rd. and Hwy. 6, on the northeast side of Kalamalka Lake. Once noted as one of the 10 most beautiful lakes in the world by *National Geographic* and referred to as "The Lake of a Thousand Colours," this park is a well-preserved remnant of the natural grasslands that once stretched from Vernon to Osoyoos. More than 10 kilometres (6 miles) of biking/ riding/hiking trails wind through the grassland slopes and along lightly forested ridges. Scenic cliff-top viewpoints overlook a rocky shoreline indented with bays and tiny coves. This park is a favourite with visitors year-round. You might glimpse coyote, deer or black bear but are more likely to see Columbian ground squirrels and yellow-bellied marmots. Pacific rattlesnakes, shy creatures that wish only to be left alone, are an important part of this fascinating ecosystem.

Kin Beach

On the eastern shore of the Vernon arm of Okanagan Lake, it offers a sandy beach, grassed areas, several picnic areas with barbecues, a large picnic shelter, change and rest rooms, a large handicapped accessible playground and boat rentals.

Kekuli Bay Provincial Park

On the west side of Kalamalka Lake, 11 kilometres (7 miles) south of Vernon, on a particularly lovely bay. The only development so far is the access road, parking lot and boat launch. The sandy beach lures visitors. A kekuli is the semi-subterranean pit house built by the Interior Natives as their winter home.

Paddlewheel Park

The 1886 terminal for the Shuswap-Okanagan Railway and today the home for the Okanagan Landing Railway Station, the Smith House and the 1892 Vernon Court House. Between Okanagan Landing Rd. and Okanagan Lake, Paddlewheel Park offers a sandy beach, grassed areas, a playground, a basketball court, sand volleyball courts, a tennis court, a boat launch and boat trailer parking.

Silver Star Mountain Resort,

1-800-663-4431, www.silverstarmtn. com (also see Skiing, page 117)

Long after the last skier has made the last run, the mountain reopens for summer with wildflower and mushroom tours by Roseanne Van Ee (545–7446, www.outdoordiscoveries.com). A chairlift takes bikers and hikers to the summit for spectacular views and exciting descents. There is also a climbing wall, horseback riding and mountain bike rentals.

Vernon Dining

Bean to Cup

3903 27th St., 503-2222, www.beantocup.com.

Enjoy a light lunch or quick cup at this multi-roomed java joint that has won numerous awards for best sandwiches and coffee.

Intermezzo
3206 34th Ave., 542-3853.

When a locally owned restaurant has been in business for more than a quarter-century you know it is doing something right. This intimate European restaurant with a slant towards Italian opens at 5 p.m. and has the appearance of a high-priced dining room, but soup, salad and main course, beautifully prepared, can be less than $15.

KT's
3127 30th Ave., 545-3228.

A downtown fixture for 30 years, this family-style pizza and pasta eatery has a row of giant saltwater aquariums to keep the kids fascinated. Fish is not a featured item on the menu. The owner is a big fan of the Survivor TV series and has special nights with prizes and contests to see who gets kicked off the island.

Pasta Garden
Best Western Vernon Lodge, 3914 32nd St., 545-3385, 1-800-663-9400, www.bestwesternvernonlodge.com/dining.

Dining beside an indoor swimming pool while a real river rushes past, just a few steps away from the tables, isn't likely to create an image of a romantic dinner. But if you separate eaters from waders with a wall of foliage that includes 10-metre (30-foot) fig trees and banana trees heavy with yellow fruit, the picture improves. Put everything inside a glass-roofed atrium and channel the river (yes, a real burbling brook that's travelling through the dining room on its way to Okanagan Lake) so that it doesn't overflow its banks in the spring, and you have a one-of-a-kind restaurant with one of the most interesting settings in the Okanagan. Excellent food and sumptuous cheesecake.

Vernon Wine

Bella Vista Vineyards,
3111 Agnew Rd., 558-0770, www.bellavista winery.ca.

COLDSTREAM | POPULATION: 9,126

Named for Coldstream Creek, which flows into Kalamalka Lake, this community feels and acts very much like a part of Vernon. Coldstream is a long, narrow valley 5 kilometres (3 miles) southeast of Vernon, with development clustered at the western end next to Kalamalka Lake. An early ranch was owned by Forbes and Charles Vernon, who sold their spread to Lord Aberdeen in 1891. Aberdeen developed orchards and subdivided the land for fellow Brits. In 2000 the Coldstream Ranch still owned agricultural land here.

LAKE COUNTRY | POPULATION: 9,750

An amalgamation of Oyama, Winfield, Okanagan Centre and Carr's Landing, Lake Country spreads along Highway 97 like a northern extension of Kelowna.

CARR'S LANDING, an orchard settlement and former steamship landing on the east side of Okanagan Lake, 20 kilometres (12 miles) southwest of Vernon, is named after Andrew Carr, an early settler who planted the area's first apple, pear and peach trees.

OKANAGAN CENTRE, with a population of 360, is a farming settlement and former steamship landing on the eastern hillsides shouldering Okanagan Lake, 20 kilometres (12 miles) north of Kelowna. A. B. Knox developed the first orchards here in the early 1900s, and a townsite, laid out in 1908, soon had a hotel, store, post office and school. Grape and wine production has become important in this area.

OYAMA, with 1,500 residents, was named after Japanese Prince Iwao Oyama, a hero in the Russo-Japanese war. Established in 1908 to serve the surrounding orchards, this settlement is barely a bump on the causeway that separates Kalamalka Lake from Wood Lake. A connecting canal runs under the road and just east of Highway 97 is a favourite spot for fishing from its bank. The clear water provides a good view of the fish you are trying to catch. Wood Lake was once a metre (three feet) higher than Kalamalka Lake, but the canal evened them out. A popular swimming area, with a sandy beach, is on the south side of the causeway and can be seen from Highway 97.

Oyama has two attractions that are about as opposite as one can imagine. One is a ramshackle building known as Okanagan Display and Store Fixtures. It has aisles of commercial shelving, racking and lighting, but stuffed in nooks and crannies are antiques, collectibles and decorator items that make rummaging fun. The other attraction is Kayola Regional Park, a peninsula that sticks out into Kalamalka Lake. A trail leads around the perimeter of the park and offers several swimming options, although the bottom is rocky everywhere except the east side. There are washrooms and change rooms, but no sign directs visitors to this developed park. Turn north on Trask Rd. and go to the end.

WINFIELD, another orchard settlement, about 30 kilometres (18 miles) south of Vernon, was named after Winfield Lodge, the home of Thomas Wood, justice of the peace, stock raiser, homesteader and the source for the name of Wood Lake. The village developed as a fruit-packing centre in the 1920s.

Lake Country Culture

Barn Gallery,
Oyama, 4450 Towgood Rd., 548-3823.
Original art and studio.

Kopje Regional Park and Gibson Heritage House,
15480 Carr's Landing Rd.

Gibson House

This lakefront acreage was purchased by George Gibson in 1906 and the house he built in 1912 is now a museum furnished in the style of the times. Self-guided tour, swimming beach, picnic area, playground and baseball diamond.

Lake Country Museum and Wentworth Cabin
In Okanagan Centre Park.

Silver Lining Studio,
15638 Oyama Rd., 548-4093.
Ceramics workshops and sales.

Tickled Pink Studio,
16392 Barkley Rd., 766-1695.
Studio with original watercolours, oils and cards by Wendy Klein.

Lake Country Wine

Arrowleaf Cellars,
1574 Camp Rd., Okanagan Centre, 766-2992, www.arrowleafcellars.com.

Gray Monk Estate Winery,
1055 Camp Rd., Okanagan Centre, 766-3168, 1-800-663-4205, www.graymonk.com.

Highway or Byway?
Oyama to Winfield

After crossing the causeway between Kalamalka Lake and Wood Lake (going east) it is a nice change of pace to stay off the highway and take the back roads almost to Kelowna. Pass through the tiny settlement of Oyama, between the lakes, and turn right (south) on Oyama Rd.

When you reach Woodsdale Rd. you can turn right (west) and shortly you will come to a park with two names: Beasley and Reiswig. There is a good sandy beach as well as change rooms, picnic facilities and a diving raft. Continuing past the park leads to Highway 97.

To stay on the back roads, don't turn on Woodsdale but continue south as Oyama Rd. changes its name to Lodge Rd. It twists and turns and soon approaches Highway 97. About 50 metres (155 feet) before reaching the highway, turn left on Bottom Wood Lake Rd. and pass a golf course, high school and a few shops. This road ends at Beaver Lake Rd., where a turn right leads to Highway 97. By going straight across the highway and following Glenmore (see Vernon to Kelowna, page 39) you reach Kelowna by the back door.

KELOWNA | POPULATION: 105,000

Kelowna is B.C.'s most populous city outside the Lower Mainland. The number of inhabitants of Greater Kelowna approaches 145,000. Victoria has more people when its metropolitan area is counted and Saanich has more residents, but it is a district, not a city. Although many would dispute the claim, it is an economic, political and demographic fact that Kelowna is the hub of the Okanagan. Its name derives from an Okanagan Native word meaning grizzly bear.

The first thing that visitors driving from the east can identify as being part of Kelowna is the floating bridge. The only bridge across Okanagan Lake is interesting, if not a thing of beauty. To locals and tourists alike the three lanes can be a bottleneck that causes congestion whenever the lift span is raised to let a big boat past, whenever a truck stalls, or a whenever a couple of cars thump bumpers. It was built as a toll bridge in 1958 and motorists contributed until 1963. There are plans for a new five-lane bridge located 4 metres (13 feet) north of the present structure, but there are many hurdles to overcome before the $100 million structure is completed in 2008.

The attraction of the present bridge is that it floats — the only one of its kind in Canada and one of very few in the world. It was done that way because of the extreme depth of the water beneath it. The new bridge is also being designed to float.

The bridge spans the narrowest part of the lake and from shore to shore is just short of 1.6 kilometres (1 mile). The floating section measures 640 metres (2,100 feet) and is constructed of pontoons that are 60 metres (200 feet) long and are submerged about 8 feet (2.2 metres). Anchors weighing 70 tons are embedded 7.5 metres (25 feet) into the lake bottom to hold everything in place. Ten regular pontoons plus two small end pontoons make up the floating section. The lift portion rises 18 metres (60 feet) above the water and is 81 metres (265 feet) long.

The second thing eastbound motorists and cyclists are likely to notice, after recovering from a hideous cluster of billboards on Westbank First Nation's land, is the large area of trees, lawns, beaches and flowers

Old bridge anchor

immediately to the left (north) on the Kelowna side of the bridge. This is City Park and anyone who has not spent an afternoon wandering through this popular greenery has not been to the heart of Urban Okanagan.

A Walk Along the Lakeshore

After crossing the bridge from Westbank, turn left and find parking

On the Lake

The *Fintry Queen*, a 155-foot (50-metre) mock sternwheeler, has been a fixture on the Kelowna waterfront since 1949 when it started life as the *Lequime*, a car ferry that shuttled vehicles across the lake before the bridge was built. Ten years later it was decommissioned and then rebuilt to resemble a paddlewheeler. Financial troubles and the requirement of an expensive inspection forced it to remain tied to the dock for two years starting in 2000. It was put up for auction on eBay but that didn't produce a buyer. In early 2003 ownership was transferred to a group from Alberta and it was refitted and a full restaurant and other features added. (979-0223, www.fintryqueen.com.)

Just before the *Fintry Queen* stopped operating, the modern Kelowna Princess (862-3138) began tours of the lake. It also docks near the foot of Bernard Ave.

on downtown streets, within the park or at a parkade two blocks from the lake on Lawrence Ave.

The two entrances to the park from Abbott St. meander through impressive rows of roses and other flowers — a botanical bevy known officially as Veendam Gardens (Veendam is one of Kelowna's sister cities — in the Netherlands). Ahead are public tennis courts, lawn bowling, a war memorial, a skateboard park and a 1955 totem pole by Oliver Jackson. Close to Highway 97 are a running track, football field, volleyball area and playing field. Children rush ahead at the sight of the water park and they aren't disappointed. There are puddles and pools, and streams of water shooting from the mouths of monsters. While a fine mist of cooling water shoots skyward, kids can climb on whales and have fun getting soaked. In front of that is a stretch of shore known as Hot Sands Beach, a name that is self-explanatory to barefooted bathers on summer afternoons.

To the left (south) a pedestrian tunnel leads under Highway 97 to a smaller beach. Public beaches are common in Kelowna. After going through the tunnel a jog left and a stroll along Abbott St. gives a glimpse of how pretty an area can be when automobile traffic is not considered to be a priority.

Following the sidewalk that runs parallel to the lake, going north from City Park, will take you past assorted artisans displaying their wares, and out of the park. The walkway leads to *The Sails,* a sculpture by R. Dow Reid that was lowered into place by helicopter in 1977. With white wings stretching skyward like a schooner reaching for wind, *The Sails* is everyone's favourite downtown meeting place and a perfect spot to people watch. When the tour busses unload, this is where the passengers head. Next to the white sculpture is the Ogopogo statue that is probably, after the lake, the most photographed item in the Okanagan. Kids love to climb on it.

Nearby, the *Fintry Queen* and the *Kelowna Princess* wait to take passengers on a nautical tour.

The small space with grass and trees in front of the Ogopogo statue is Kerry Park, where musicians perform many evenings of the summer. The names of many of Kelowna's waterfront spots, such as Hot Sands Beach and Tugboat Bay, are spread by word of mouth and are not signposted.

The lakeshore path expands to a divided way, separating pedestrians from human-powered wheeled transport, and passes the new Stuart Park and the yacht club before reaching the Grand Hotel.

Inside the luxurious Grand Okanagan Lakefront Resort and Conference Centre (the hotel's full name, but usually called

"The Grand"), is a classy array of shops and a restaurant that face a statue of three black dolphins cavorting in a fountain that is the centre-piece of the hotel's lobby. The sculpture, *Harmony*, by R. Dow Reid, compares to his white dolphins, *Rhapsody*, which cavort in a nearby out- door fountain.

Kelowna's brochure lists the central Okanagan's only casino, an adjunct to The Grand, as a cultural district attraction, but you won't find it described in that context here.

Walking behind the hotel and keeping to the shore of the lake, the sidewalk crosses what is likely one of the world's smallest nautical locks. Boaters coming in from the lake call on a phone for a "lock-smith" to come and open the gates to flood the short canal and bring their boat up a metre (three feet) or so to the same level as the lagoon. The tiny lock is about 10 metres (33 feet) long and 3.5 metres (10 feet) wide. Waterfront Park occupies most of what is behind The Grand and it features a wonderful kilometre or two (a mile or so) of paths with gardens, waterfalls, the Island Stage, lagoons and a board-walk.

Emerging at the north end, after following the boardwalk along the shore, you will find, appropriately placed beside a sandy beach known as Tugboat Bay, a bronze sculpture called *On the Beach*, by Kelowna sculptor Geert Maas. When locals refer to a sculpture called *The Sunbathers*, this is what they are talking about.

Along this waterfront walkway an interesting array of activities awaits intrepid tourists, travellers and residents. These range from renting an Ogopogo paddleboat to parasailing hundreds of feet above the lake. Other possibilities include rentals of sail, paddle or power-boats, bicycle rentals, airplane rides, water skiing and lake tours.

The city offers free summertime walking tours of the historical parts of downtown, departing from *The Sails* at 10 a.m., noon and 1:30 p.m. Brochures for self-guided walking tours are available at tourist information stops.

After touring Waterfront Park and The Grand, if you have seen enough of the lakeshore, pass between the two low buildings (concession building and wash-rooms) and follow the path over Harmony Bridge to the dolphins statue, where you can take the downtown "cultural district" tour (described ahead).

Otherwise, continue along the lakeshore behind the new Discovery Bay condos and through the Brandt's Creek nature area where you may see a great blue heron, osprey or any number of ducks and, of course,

The Sails

Silhouetted trees in City Park

the ubiquitous Canada goose. Boardwalks lead out to the Rotary Marsh Wildlife Sanctuary, with viewing areas and information signs.

The main pathway crosses Sunset Dr., goes under an Oriental-style entry and then follows Brandt's Creek to Recreation Ave. A great blue heron wading in the creek may catch your eye, but look again — it's a sculpture. A jog right, at the end of the path, leads to Ellis St. A right turn on Ellis will take you past the library and museums, described next, to Bernard Ave. and The Sails sculpture at the lake.

If you are on two wheels, or if you are an enthusiastic hiker, a left turn on Ellis St. paves the way to Knox Mountain or even to Paul's Tomb, both of which are described under cycling/hiking.

Kelowna Downtown Cultural District

Kelowna has reached the point in its artistic growth where there are enough museums and galleries clustered downtown to boast a "cultural district." Within this area, bordered by the lake, Clement Ave. to the north, Queensway to the south and Ellis St., there are about a dozen sites of interest, plus numerous works of art. Here is a quick walkthrough, with mentions of a few points that are not necessarily culturally significant. Start at the north end of Water St. where it curves around the big arena called Prospera Place (named by a financial institution). When the Western Hockey League and Memorial Cup champion Kelowna Rockets aren't playing, the 6,000-seat arena, built in 1999, has hosted the likes of Elton John, Rod Stewart and Jose Carreras. Opposite the arena, on the other side of Water St., is the sculpture of entwined dolphins formally titled Rhapsody. It's a favourite north-end meeting place and marks the entrance to Waterfront Park and Tugboat Bay.

Cawston Ave. runs between Ellis and Water streets. At the Water/ Cawston corner sits the Kelowna Art Gallery (1315 Water St., 762-2226). Programs and displays are constantly changing. Admission is free after 3 p.m. Thursday.

At 421 Cawston, 717-5304, sits the new Rotary Centre for the Arts (RCA), near the Art Gallery. Dancers, artists and musicians rehearse in rooms that are open to public view. There are pottery studios, artisans' rooms and music rooms as well as a theatre, cafe and offices. The Alternator Gallery for Contemporary Art (868-2298, www.alternatorgallery.com) is located here. Established in 1988 as a non-profit artist-run centre, the Alternator displays the works of students and professionals and provides a venue for unorthodox or controversial art not exhibited in municipal or commercial galleries. There is no admission charge to the Rotary Centre so you can't go wrong by wandering through this fascinating place and, at a minimum, enjoying the architecture and artwork on display. Investigate both floors and go to the ends of the corridors and around the corners. There is more than meets the eye and volunteer guides are often on duty to give tours.

At 1304 Ellis at Cawston the Laurel Packinghouse contains the British Columbia Orchard Industry Museum, 763-0433, often referred to as the Apple Museum, and the B.C. Wine Museum, 868-0441, and wine shop. The Laurel Packinghouse, Kelowna's first designated heritage building, dates to 1917 when it was a shipping house for orchard products. Parts of the original structure are still visible inside. The Wine Museum sells wine from nearly every Okanagan winery and will offer a taste. Items displayed for sale far outweigh museum displays, making the name a little misleading, but for the oenophile it's a must. Across the hall, the Orchard Museum has a visitor-operated, 16-metre (50-foot) model train setup, a re-creation of an old packinghouse and lots of artefacts. It owns a stock of original old apple box labels that it sells. No admission charge.

Packinghouses

Packinghouses that have been converted to other uses are not unusual in the Okanagan. According to historian James H. Hayes, 50 years ago there were 19 of the sturdy, insulated buildings used to store fruit before it was shipped out. Today, he says, just three continue to carry out their original function: B.C. Fruit Packers Co-operative, Okanagan North Growers Co-operative and Sun-Fresh Co-operative Growers.

Opposite the Rotary Arts Centre, on Cannery Lane, next to the arena, sits The Art Ark, 862-5080, comprised of three interconnecting galleries and a fine-arts boutique. There is a huge array of first-class paintings, pottery, photographs, prints, sculptures, crafts and more. Next door the Turtle Island Gallery showcases the best of First Nation's artwork and crafts. Set aside at least an hour to enjoy these two emporia.

Back across Cawston and behind the Centre for the Arts is something called

Apple boxes at the Orchard Museum

both an artwalk and a pergola. The definition of the latter is an arbour or a passageway of columns supporting a roof of trelliswork on which climbing plants are trained to grow. It will be a few years before the vines grow to the overhangs of the metal lattices but, even though shade is scarce, the mosaics of old apple box advertising and sculptures of fruit make this an exceptionally pleasant walkway that leads from the Rotary Centre to the enigmatic public library on Ellis St. This beautiful building, said by some to resemble an open book, has a sparse interior and looks like it could use more books.

Across from the library sits an interesting cluster of shops selling water gardens, interior and exterior home decor and art supplies. The Kelowna Actor's Studio is another former apple storage warehouse that has been transformed into a theatre. It also houses acting and musical theatre classes.

On Ellis St. pass Memorial Arena, which has been largely replaced by Prospera Place. In size and architecture, it is typical of hundreds of post-World War II hockey arenas built in smaller Canadian cities. The Okanagan Military Museum is here, open Tuesday, Thursday and Saturday from 10 a.m. to 4 p.m. Artefacts, memorabilia and exhibits about Canadian military from 1899.

The Kelowna Museum, 763-2417, at the corner of Queensway and Ellis, displays human and natural history from the Okanagan region. Exhibits change periodically. An interesting recent one explained the role of the Chinese in Kelowna's history. No admission charge.

Kelowna Library

Around the corner and past the bus terminal on Queensway, an imposing clock chimes out the hours. The Bennett Clock honours former B.C. premier W.A.C. (Wacky) Bennett, who lived much of his life in Kelowna. The carillon clock's 20 pillars signify Bennett's 20 years as premier and the seven steps relate to the number of terms he was in office.

Hidden behind both city hall and the clock is a treasure you are unlikely to uncover without some guidance. Kasugai Gardens symbolizes the friendship between sister cities Kelowna and Kasugai, Japan. The tranquil Japanese-style garden with ponds, bridges and plump koi swimming happily, provides a perfect place for a brown-bag lunch or a moment of Zen contemplation.

From the Gardens, a walkway beside city hall (built in 1949) leads back to Water St. and on the opposite side, the swaying masts of the boats at the private Kelowna Yacht Club. To the right, on Water St., is the 900-seat Kelowna Community Theatre (1962), home to the Okanagan Symphony and Sunshine

Bennett Clock

Theatre. The lobby usually displays local artwork, 762-2471.

This cultural tour ends close to where it began, but Kelowna culture continues beyond the downtown district.

Fruit Packers Co-operative

The Apple Core

A different kind of culture is found by walking up Clement Ave. (Water St. curves around the new arena and more or less becomes Clement) to the B.C. Fruit Packers Co-operative where a dozen or more varieties of apples are sold for considerably less than at the supermarket. If you are curious about the taste of a certain variety just ask for a sample. Those who are making apple juice or baking pies head for the back and pick through the reduced-price "juicers."

Souvenir apple.

Continue up Clement to where it ends at Gordon, turn left and then left again on Weddel Pl. and stop at the Sun-Rype factory. Fruit juice that is close to expiry date, overstocked items and damaged items are sold from a warehouse at reduced prices. Hefty bags of fruit leathers are usually available. The small bars that normally retail for 40 cents each can be bought in bulk for less than 10 cents apiece. The quantity of juice varies with the season and the reason. The hours of operation also change, but normally you can count on Wednesday to Friday from 10 a.m. to 3 p.m.

More Kelowna Culture, Education and Amusements

Elysium Gardens

Lake City Casinos, Grand Hotel
1300 Water St., 860-9467, www.lakecitycasinos.com.
As well as 20,000 square feet of slots and games, the casino boasts the only escalator in Kelowna.

Blueberry Hill Gallery
4000 Glenmore Rd. N., 766-0525,
www. viviansworld.com.
Vivian Kuhn's vivid and amusing art is created in the studio in her log home.

Elysium Garden-Nursery
2834 Belgo Rd., 491-1368,
www.elysiumgardennursery. com.
The Okanagan's only commercial display garden features thousands of perennials in an old apple orchard near the rushing Mission Creek. The owners started planting in 1998 with the idea of showing the range of flowers that can be grown in the Okanagan. The 1.3 beautiful and bountiful hectares (3 acres) include a Japanese garden, xeriscape garden, nursery, plant sales and self-guided tours.

Farmers' Markets
Two markets compete in Kelowna. The longest-running is the Kelowna Farmers' and Crafters' Market at Springfield Rd. and Dilworth Dr. next to the mall. Up to 165 vendors and 5,000 customers converge on Saturday mornings, starting at 8 a.m. The market also runs on summer Wednesday mornings with fewer vendors. The Downtown Market is a recent addition, with 25 vendors selling in the Prospera Place parking lot on Water St. starting at 8 a.m. on Saturdays.

Father Pandosy Mission
3685 Benvoulin Rd., 860-8369.
This is the earliest European settlement in the Valley and, with four of the original buildings still intact, it is a historical gem. The Mission was established during the fall and winter of 1859–60 by Fathers Charles Pandosy and Pierre Richard, two Oblate Catholic missionaries. Later they were joined by John MacDougall, the first outside trader, who married a Native woman. The settlers opened the Valley's first school and church. The original buildings are the Brother's House, the Chapel, the Root House and the Barn. The Christian House (named after the Christian family) and a log cabin have been moved to the site. Self-guided tour with brochure is available.

Geert Maas Sculpture Gardens and Gallery
250 Reynolds Rd., 860-7012, www. geertmaas.org.

If you like the downtown On the Beach sculpture—and who wouldn't—there is much more of Geert Maas's work on display at his studio. Visitors can stroll among bronze, stone, steel and aluminum artwork outside and enjoy oils, acrylics, lacquers and smaller sculptures inside.

Guisachan Heritage Park
1060 Cameron.

In Gaelic that difficult word means "Place of the Firs." If you pronounce it something like gooshigan or geeshigan and say it quickly no one will laugh at you, for there is no consistency in local pronunciation. Unfortunately, the firs didn't like the Okanagan climate and died off. The house was built for Lady Aberdeen in 1891 and has many of the features of a colonial bungalow. Perennial gardens surround the house, with many flowers planted by various owners of the property. There are 110 varieties of roses, 30 types of herbs, 50 species of trees, 30 different shrubs, 150 perennials and 25 annuals, as well as the shaded avenue of the cedars. The log house on the site was built in the late 1870s. There is a restaurant in the main house plus the Milkshed Gift Shop. No admission charge. Watch for the flower show at the beginning of July.

Hambleton Galleries
781 Bernard Ave., 860-2498, www.hambletongalleries.com.

Jack and Lorna Hambleton have been displaying artwork in Kelowna since 1964. Their gallery is in a heritage home built by the Leckie family in 1906.

Kelowna Land and Orchard Company (KLO)
3002 Dunster Rd., 763-1091, www.k-l-o.com.

This 60-hectare (150-acre) working farm and commercial apple orchard, 15 minutes from downtown Kelowna, produces 2.5 million kilograms (6 million pounds) of fruit annually. British Columbia, incidentally, grows 30 percent of Canadian apples. The orchard was established in 1904 and now has a petting zoo, tours of the orchard, fresh apple juice, Teahouse Restaurant and lots of informative signage for those who want to take an unguided tour.

A new part of the complex is Raven Ridge Cidery, which is producing high-end apple ciders that are consumed as wines and champagnes.

Pandosy Mission

Grand Prix Fun Centre, miniature car racing and games
911 Stremel Rd., 765-1434.

Okanagan Lavender Herb Farm,
4380 Takla Rd., 764-7795, www. okanaganlavender.com.
As well as the scents, visitors enjoy self-guided tours, self-pick and gift shop. A harvest festival is held in early July and a Christmas Fair is in winter. Sixty varieties of lavender are grown here. It's set in an area of rolling vineyards, orchards and gigantic homes, so sightseeing is an adventure.

Roger D. Arndt Studio and Exhibition Salon
1555B Teasdale Rd., 765-9568.
Among Kelowna's apple orchards is nestled an artist-inspired architectural creation where Roger D. Arndt paints his landscapes.

Scandia
2898 Highway 97 N., 765-2355, www.scandiagolfand games.com.
Indoor and outdoor mini-golf, beautiful flowered gardens, 130 video and skill games, bumper cars, batting cages and kids' rides.

Thunder Mountain Raceway
on Highway 33, 40 kilometres (25 miles) southeast of Kelowna, 763-7358, www.thundermountainraceway. com,
Features a $^1/8$-mile drag strip with electronics, concession and grandstands. Race classes include Top Comp, Super Pro, Sportsman, Snow machine/Bike, Novice and Junior Dragster.

Dancing Pedestrians
by Jock Hildebrand

OKANAGAN LiTE:
Teens Are Shooting at Me With Guns

I hid behind a tree, raised a gun and shot a young man.

Normally I'm against guns. I'm opposed to pretend guns in the hands of children, virtual guns in the hands of video game players and staple guns in the hands of the uncoordinated. I'm scared by stun guns, soldering guns and glue guns.

The young man I shot was, officially, dead, although he shouted, "Hit," raised his right arm and marched away. He wore a yellow splotch of paint that I felt good about having applied. We were playing paintball.

It was my son's birthday so, despite my ethical protests, we headed to Safari Ridge, between Kelowna and Westbank. My son is still rebelling over being the only kid on the block who didn't get mock Terminator armament for Christmas. He carries a paintball gun the size of a lawnmower and in 10 seconds can coat the town of Peachland in $200 worth of paint.

In the paintball world of pretend war, 5 to 20 young men (and occasionally a young woman and, rarely, an older gentleman) dress in camouflage outfits, or coveralls, and go to opposite ends of a war zone, which is festooned with walls, ditches, fences and logs. Each combatant is armed with a gun that fires marble-sized paintballs 100 metres (330 feet) per second and leaves a welt the size of a plate on any skin not covered by three layers of thick clothing. Their mothers' admonishments of "You'll put someone's eye out," are thwarted by a facemask.

The object is to capture a flag, but mostly people just shoot each other. The recipient of a splat of paintball dies and has an obligation to leave the playing area.

Safari Ridge Paintball

When the battle began, my comrades-in-arms raced off to attack the enemy and I didn't know what to do. The referee had not explained the procedure for being a conscientious objector, so I cowered behind a broken wall while enemy fire exploded all around me. If I ran away and deserted, would my own team shoot me? My heart was pounding and I was sweating. This was play? I tried to imagine the terror a real soldier must feel in battle.

My mock-soldier comrades were shouting "Hit" and pathetically raising an arm as they marched to the sidelines. I crouched lower to avoid the splatting paint, but the inevitable happened — a ball found its way through an opening and burst on my shoulder. Ouch! A yellow streak down my back would have been more appropriate. A horn sounded — we had been slaughtered. Names like Culloden, Waterloo and Little Big Horn came to mind.

As my team members reloaded, I pretended to do the same. At 10 cents per paintball this wasn't costing much — I had yet to find a target.

Round two went much the same as the first, but in round three I managed to spend half a buck firing a few rounds in the general direction of some menacing shrubbery. Some new recruits helped us make forays into enemy territory and at last I came upon one of the green vermin sniping at our courageous warriors. When I saw the whites of his eyes I fired and hit him squarely on the ankle. An official kill! I grabbed my pocket-knife and ran forward but my son grabbed me and demanded, "What are you doing?"

"I'm going to get his scalp," I exclaimed.

At the end of four hours of mock war my legs were stiff from running for cover. When you are terror-stricken, you don't appreciate the quality of the exercise.

Those who are inspired by my bravado can find paintball battlefields in Penticton, Westbank and Vernon.

Kids Behind the Wheel

Children aged three to eight are getting behind the wheel and taking their first driving lessons. They stop at red lights, yield to pedestrians, make safe turns and buckle their seat belts. The cars they drive are powered by their own legs and the streets are miniaturized versions of the real thing.

Every year, at the Little Traveller's Safety Village, in the Rutland section of Kelowna, thousands of children enjoy taking on adult responsibilities as 30 brightly coloured pedal cars manoeuvre the streets. The students also take a 30-minute classroom course in traffic safety and then practice crossing the street, walking facing traffic and looking out for automobiles.

In Penticton, a similar miniature village focusses on bicycle safety. The streets pass a Safety House, fire station, intersections and lots of traffic signs. There is no charge at either Safety Village and bookings in Kelowna are not necessary in the summer months. There are two sessions, starting at 10 a.m. and at 2 p.m. Appointments must be made in Penticton.

Little Traveller's Safety Village, 395 Hartman Rd. Kelowna (Rutland), 765-3163, www.kdsc.bc.ca.

Penticton Safety Village, 490 Edmonton Ave., 493-8883.

Kelowna Dining

Eating out in the Okanagan is almost always a casual affair. Even the snootiest restaurants accept customers wearing shorts and sandals in the middle of summer. A garment that covers the area from neck to umbilicus is, however, generally required on both men and women.

Guisachan House
1060 Cameron, 862-9368, www.worldclasscatering.com.

Set amid perfect gardens in Guisachan Heritage Park, this restaurant, the former home of Lord and Lady Aberdeen, offers one of the best lunch deals in town. For less than $10 one can enjoy top-quality soup, salad, entree and dessert while watching the hummingbirds seek nectar among the profusion of flowers. The evening menu is one of the most extensive in the Okanagan, with more than 90 selections.

Lena's Pancake House
533 Bernard Ave., 861-5531.

The minute you walk in the door you know there is something different here. It's the smoke — not burning pancakes, but cigarettes. Since the owners are the only employees, smoking is permitted. If you want to puff at your plate, this is the place to do it. Is the food good? Does it matter if your taste buds are asphyxiated?

Teahouse Restaurant
3002 Dunster Rd., 712-9404, www.k-l-o.com/ teahouse.

On a dead-end road, atop a hill overlooking the Valley, this orchard eatery has a patio that offers a most enjoyable panoramic view of Kelowna and the lake. It is part of KLO Orchards, which offers walking tours for those wishing to take a stroll before or after dinner. The apple juice and ice apple wine alone are worth the trip. The daunting array of beverages includes 20 varieties of tea.

The Finer Choice
237 Lawrence Ave., 763-0422.

One of the best deals in fine dining in the Okanagan occurs here between 5 and 6 p.m., when a superb meal of soup or salad, main course and dessert is served for about $12.50, half the usual price.

Nishi's Japanese Restaurant
272 Bernard Ave., 862-8818.

This Japanese restaurant seats you on cushions on the floor in private tatami rooms, or on traditional western chairs. Best buy is the Lunch Box, served, of course, at lunchtime. Less than $10 for soup and a compartmentalized tray with 8 to 10 different foods, each with a distinct flavour.

Vintropolis Tapas Bar
321 Bernard Ave., 762-7682.

Kelowna's first tapas bar proffers a unique combination of wines and exotic appetizers. There is much ado about matching wine and meal, and one can try a Vin Flight, three small glasses of wine on a silver tray. Comfortable seats, quiet background music and subtle lighting encourage conversation in an interesting downtown location.

Wild Apple Grill
at Manteo Beach Resort, 3762 Lakeshore Rd., 860-4488.

With patio seating on the edge of the lake and an abundance of huge windows, this is the place to watch the sun set behind the mountains while dining. A dozen dazzling flavours enhance every plate and a single decadent dessert feeds a hungry pair.

Kelowna Wine

Calona Vineyards
1125 Richter St., 762-9144, www.calona.kelowna. com.

Cedar Creek Estate Winery
5445 Lakeshore Rd., 764-8866, www.cedar creek.bc.ca.

House Of Rose Winery
2270 Garner Rd., 765-0802, www.winterwine. com.

Pinot Reach Cellars
1670 Dehart Rd., 764-0078, www.pinotreach. com.

St. Hubertus Estate Winery
5225 Lakeshore Rd., 764-7888, www.st- hubertus.bc.ca.

Summerhill Pyramid Winery
4870 Chute Lake Rd., 764-8000, www. summerhill.bc.ca.

WESTBANK | POPULATION: 36,000

For the purposes of this book, Westbank and the Westside will be considered synonymous. They comprise the area between the only bridge over Okanagan Lake and the Glenrosa interchange on Highway 97, where the road leads to Crystal Mountain Ski Resort.

Highway or Byway?
Kelowna through Westbank

Every day, tens of thousands of automobiles rush through Westbank and their drivers give little consideration to Highway 97 alternatives. Heading west, go 2.5 kilometres (1.5 miles) after crossing the bridge from Kelowna, then turn towards the lake (left) at the lights onto Boucherie Rd. After going downhill you reach a tranquil stretch of lakeside road favoured by cyclists and pedestrians. This route takes twice as long, probably longer, because you will be tempted to stop for a swim, take a short walk beside a rolling river or enjoy a tasting at a winery. Wineries you pass on this route are Slamka, Mt. Boucherie and Quails' Gate, and, just off the route, Mission Hill.

You will follow about three kilometres (two miles) of lakeshore with a jogging/biking path beside it and plenty of picnic tables. A right turn from Boucherie onto Gellatly Rd. can quickly take you to the hustle of downtown Westbank. But what's the hurry? Keep going on Boucherie as the name changes to Gellatly Rd., which is shaped like a giant "U" connecting to Highway 97 in two places. You'll see Gellatly Bay Aquatic Park, Kent Park and Rotary Park. Near where Powers Creek enters the lake, opposite the boat launch and yacht club, there is a pleasant nature walk with wooden bridges spanning the creek. Along Whitworth Rd. the Gellatly Nut Farm is being developed as an historical site and Heritage Regional Park. The log house and barn have been restored and a trail winds through the 3-hectare (7-acre) nut farm. Continuing along Boucherie (now Gellatly) the road follows the creek and at a curve in the road you'll come to a beautiful oasis with a small waterfall. The road continues up some steep hills to join Highway 97 at the Glenrosa intersection, having completely bypassed Westbank.

Westbank Amusements, Culture and Education

Jassmann Studio,
2738 Lower Glenrosa Rd., next to the Westbank Museum, 768-5547.
B. J. Jassmann has been involved with porcelain for some 20 years.

19 Greens,
2050 Campbell Rd., 769-0213, www.19greenskelowna. com.
A par 62, 18-hole putting course, a trampoline and a climbing wall.

Rasa Gallery,
3339 Gellatly Rd., 768-0633, www.jockhildebrand. com.
The work of sculptor Jock Hildebrand is created and displayed at the Rasa Gallery, located in an old apple-packing warehouse overlooking Okanagan Lake. Rasa, in Sanskrit, describes the energy between a work of art and its viewer.

Safari Ridge Paintball,
Horizon Dr., 769-0239, www.safariridge.com.
Rentals of all paintball equipment and short games suited to experts and beginners. Soaker games using water guns are played in the summer months. Electronic scoring is used.

Westside Go-Karts,
768-6877, 2101 Old Okanagan Hwy., www.westsidegokarts.com.

Waterslide,
Mariner's Reef, 2101 Old Okanagan Hwy., 768-5141,
www.welcometokelowna.com/marinersreef

Okanagan's largest waterslide park. Two twister slides, quad slide, river ravine ride, two intermediate slides, three children's slides, hot tub, and a playground and RV park.

Westbank Museum,

2736 Lower Glenrosa Rd., 768-0110, www.okanagan.net/wmuseum.
Displayed are close to 4,000 pioneer artefacts collected from around the world, many relating to the Westbank area.

Westbank Pottery Studio,
at Paynter's Market, 101 – 2565 Main St. (Highway 97), 768-3722.
Features the work of Gillian Paynter, plus stoneware and pottery.

Westbank Wine

Mission Hill Family Estate Winery,
1730 Mission Hill Rd., 768-7611, www.missionhillwinery.com.

Mt. Boucherie Estate Winery,
829 Douglas Rd., 769-8803, www.mtboucherie.bc.ca.

Quails' Gate Estate Winery,
3303 Boucherie Rd., 769-4451, www.quailsgate.com.

Slamka Cellars Winery,
2815 Ourtoland Rd., 769-0404, www.slamka.bc.ca.

Highway or Byway?
Westbank to Vernon, 97 Alternative
For most of this publication, routes are described from north to south. In this case travel is described in the opposite direction because this route appeals to those arriving in the Okanagan via the Connector, or going to Vernon from Westbank.

This 90-kilometre (55-mile) route goes up the west side of Okanagan Lake past Bear Creek, through Fintry and across Highway 97 to Vernon. To follow this route to Westbank from Vernon, go northwest on Highway 97, follow the signs south to Fintry and enjoy the sights in the reverse order to which they are described.

From Westbank, go towards Kelowna on Highway 97 and turn left at the lights onto West Side Rd. From Kelowna, cross the floating bridge and turn right at the lights onto West Side Rd. (also spelled Westside), and you are on your way.

West Side Rd. starts off reasonably wide, but soon narrows and becomes a twisting black ribbon of asphalt dribbled along the hillside abutting the lake. Tourists in big RVs, loggers in huge trucks and rubbernecking locals provide the ingredients, and the terrain is a recipe for disaster. And disasters do happen. A moment's inattention and you could be rolling down 50 metres (160 feet) of unguarded cliff. So drive carefully and cautiously.

Despite the fact that it is scenic and rural and not heavily travelled after the first 15 kilometres (9 miles), this isn't a great cycling route. There is not so much as a cycling white line or a paved shoulder, let alone a cycling lane. Nevertheless, the viewpoints are superb and the road passes Native communities, provincial parks, recreational developments and historic sights.

The Laird of Fintry

Fintry sits on a river delta that James Cameron Dun-Waters named after his estate in Stirlingshire, Scotland. Dun-Waters, a wealthy Scotsman, came to B.C. in 1908 to pursue his passion for hunting and was so impressed with the North Okanagan that he sold the estate he had inherited and, between 1910 and 1930, bought much of the land in the Fintry area. With his wife and a few servants, he did a remarkable job of developing the area into his personal empire.

He used nearby waterfalls to generate electricity for the property, initiated his own 7-line telephone exchange and built an irrigation system. He constructed barns for pigs, horses and cattle that he fed with grain grown on land at a higher altitude.

Using local brick and stone he built an eight-room house that is now a museum. The house contained all the luxuries of the time and had the finest fittings. Outside there was a putting green, tennis court and curling rink. Paddlewheelers on the lake made frequent stops at the manor. In 1914 Dun-Waters, at age 50, joined the Middlesex Yeomanry as a captain and saw World War I action in Italy, Gallipoli and Africa.

When the estate was in full production, Dun-Waters

CONTINUES ON PAGE 63

Once on West Side Rd., almost immediately to the right is Old Ferry Wharf Rd. The name says it all. Before a bridge was built across Okanagan Lake, the ferry that traversed the lake's narrowest point docked here with cars and cargo. Some of the old wharf remains, and it is a favourite for teens who like to dive from the pilings. The adjacent campgrounds are on Native-owned land.

After 8 kilometres (5 miles) along West Side Rd., you reach Bear Creek Provincial Park, a popular campground and a pleasant place to picnic and swim. Across the road from the park is a parking area with interpretive signs and the start of hiking trails. You can follow a trail along Bear Creek to a waterfall that is impressive in the spring but becomes a trickle in autumn.

Continuing along West Side Rd. you pass beside, and through, several points of interest.

Marmot at Lake Okanagan Resort

Lake Okanagan Resort

(2751 Westside Rd. 1-800-663-3273, www.lake okanagan.com)

Features tennis courts, swimming pools, hot tubs, a fitness centre, a golf course, horseback riding, boat rentals, rooms and an excellent restaurant with a view to dine for. This is the only Okanagan summer tourist accommodation that truly fits the definition "destination resort," although several lay claim to such status. The high-ceilinged, glass-walled Chateau dining room gives a superb panorama of the lake and at night the lights of Kelowna twinkle in the distance. The food is as good as the view, with fine cuisine served to the highest European standards. The resort owns 1.6 kilometres (1 mile) of shoreline and 120 hectares (300 acres) of land crossed by hiking and riding trails.

Marmots, overgrown golden gophers, are the scourge of golf courses. If you want to have a look at the playful little critters without playing 18 holes, you can stop beside the golf course. The chances are excellent that one will pop its head up in the middle of the fairway or from beneath the roots of a tree. Even if you have no intention of eating or staying at the resort the architecture and layout is worth a quick diversion.

The Stables (769-2634)

At the north end, famous for its trail rides, which end at the lake and give riders an opportunity to hold onto the mane or the tail of a swimming horse and be pulled along for a unique ride.

Ridgeview RV Resort

Farther along West Side Rd.,

Trail ride ends with a swim

the resort spreads over a steep hillside facing the lake. This huge development for recreational vehicles reaches down to the lake and has about 500 lots.

Fintry (more properly, Fintry Delta)
Thirty-three kilometres (21 miles) from the bridge, at the mouth of Short's Creek.

A relatively new provincial park next to the town includes the usual picnicking, swimming and camping spots, but this is recreation with an historical flavour. It's hard to believe, but this site was once the transportation hub of the Valley: Hudson's Bay Company fur traders passed through here and steamers docked daily on their routes around the lake. A walking trail will take you to the waterfalls and deep pools of Short's Creek, as well as a suspension bridge and the remains of irrigation and power generation structures. Other features from the past include part of a ferry wharf from which freight boats operated, a preserved manor house, a caretaker's house and several barns, including a rare octagonal one that is under restoration.

Shortly after Fintry, West Side Rd. passes through property of the Okanagan Indian Band and then meets Highway 97, where a right turn takes you past O'Keefe Ranch to a junction with Highway 97A, between Armstrong and Vernon. Turn right for Vernon.

PEACHLAND | POPULATION: 5,000
When John Moore Robinson, in 1897, tasted the local peaches and realized the area's agricultural potential, he developed it as the first of three communities that he would found in the Okanagan.

Robinson had made his fortune in the newspaper business in central Canada when he decided to head west in search of gold during the Klondike gold rush of the late 1800s. Stopping briefly in the Okanagan he succumbed to the beauty and climate and realized the potential of the area. After surveying and developing the townsites of Peachland and Summerland, as well as many orchards, he set his sights on Naramata, near Penticton.

The best thing about pretty little Peachland is its shoreline: nearly 4 kilometres (2.5 miles) of public lakeshore with docks, grass, picnic tables, a boat launch, trees, sand, marina, a kids' playground and the only lifeguards on an Okanagan beach. All the homes and commercial buildings are on the west side of the main thoroughfare, while the lake side is public land.

Squally Point, in Okanagan Mountain Park, is directly across the lake from Peachland and is said to be the home of Ogopogo. Keep your eyes sharp and your camera ready. Driving through Peachland is a pleasant deviation from busy Highway 97. There are several entry points to the town. After passing the turnoff for

became ill with cancer. It was deep into the Depression and he could find no buyer for his property.

With no children to leave it to, he sold it to a London charity for $1.

Many poor English children subsequently visited the manor and learned about rural Canadian life. He died in 1939.

In 1995 the BC government bought the estate as a provincial park, and in 1996 a 130-site campground was added. His home is open for tours and has been restored to its former elegance. In the trophy room are numerous antelope heads, a full giraffe head and neck and a Kodiak bear that Dun-Waters shot. Fifty years ago the bear was donated to the Kelowna Museum. For decades the museum basement was its home and children climbed on its back and had their pictures taken. When the Fintry house was restored, the bear was returned.

Kodiak bear displayed at Fintry

the highway to Vancouver, just south of Westbank, descend the hill and turn left, following the signs for camping. At the lake, turn right. You are on Beach Ave., the main street, and continuing south will lead you through Peachland and back onto 97. But first take time to enjoy the main street.

Hardy Falls

Peachland Amusements, Culture, Education and Nature

Antlers Beach
Beside the lake, about 5 kilometres (3 miles) south of town, Antlers Beach provides picnic tables and a place to swim. A sign commemorates a 1998 Wildlife Fence that stretches from Summerland to Peachland alongside the highway and has prevented many automobile collisions with deer. It is stated that deer come as many as 70 kilometres (45 miles) from the Merritt area to winter by the warmer lake.

Hardy Falls
On a hot summer day, this is the only place in Peachland that is as good as the beach. About 4 kilometres (2.5 miles) south of town (on Highway 97) turn right (away from the lake) at the start of Antlers Beach Recreation Area, and stop after less than 100 metres (330 feet). A 10-minute walk alongside Deep Creek, on a path that crosses the twisting creek eight times on bridges, takes you to Hardy Falls. The 10-metre (33-foot) falls fills a gorge with cool mist and you can wade in the rocky creek bed below the cataract. Dippers fly past and roost in the rocks on the hillside. Harry Hardy was one of the first orchardists in the area.

Okanagan Pottery Studio
6030 Highway 97, 767-2010, www.okanaganpottery.com.
This cottage-like building beside the highway just south of Peachland has operated as a studio since it was constructed in 1968.

Parrot Island visitor feeds orphan bird

Parrot Island Sanctuary
5090 MacKinnon Rd., 767-9030 www.parrotisland.net.
Ray and Val Parkes provide homes for several dozen parrots that have been abandoned, neglected or just given to them because the owners grew tired of the long-living pets. They give guided tours and demonstrations. Donation asked.

Peachland 1910 Museum
At the south end of town on Beach Ave., exhibits artefacts and photographs that depict the history of the district. The museum is a former Baptist Church, an unusual eight-sided wooden building constructed in 1910. Across the street stands an unmarked totem pole and, slightly south, a nice mural decorates the retaining wall beside the street.

Castle on a Cliff

Just south of Peachland, looking down on Highway 97, sits Cara Castle, also called Fantasy Inn (6239 Highway 97, 767-3124). It used to be called Castle Haymour after its owner Eddy Haymour, who also owned Rattlesnake Island, the only real island in Okanagan Lake, opposite Peachland. The island blends in with the hills behind and is hard to see from the shoreline but from higher elevations it stands out.

The story of Mr. Haymour and his island is so weird and diverse that the point where the truth and prevarication intersect is blurred. He was either a deranged terrorist or a misunderstood benefactor. Here are the two versions.

Benevolent Eddy Haymour

Eddy Haymour came to Edmonton from Lebanon as a young man, did well in business and moved to the Okanagan in 1969. Looking to create a tourist attraction that would blend cultures and display Arab traditions he bought two-hectare (five-acre) Rattlesnake Island in 1971. As he built his cultural attraction, government red tape became tighter and tighter, but he managed to open the partially completed site and 700 attended. Government bureaucracy prevented him from completing it, however he relentlessly fought back. Ultimately the government retaliated with its final weapon — it committed him to a mental institution for a 15-day evaluation and then kept him there for almost a year, although doctors said he was not disturbed. His mail was kept from him, and after his insurance lapsed, his huge house, complete with elevator, mysteriously burned. While in the institution he had to sell his island to the government. Shortly after the sale he was released.

He returned to his homeland and, with his brothers, schemed to have these injustices righted. At the Canadian embassy in Lebanon he took hostages and demanded nothing more than a fair trial. When he was promised his day in court, the event ended without harm.

The trial dragged on for seven years, but finally Mr. Haymour was awarded a written apology and financial compensation.

He purchased property south of Peachland, opposite his beloved island, and built a fabulous hotel that welcomed guests from all over the world. He wrote his biography, From Nuthouse to Castle (available over the Internet), and sold the hotel in 1994. The story of his ordeal has played on British Columbia stages.

Haymour the Nuthouse Terrorist

After making some quick money in Edmonton, Lebanese Eddy Haymour moved to the Okanagan in 1969 and bought up the only island in Okanagan Lake with plans to turn it into a tacky tourist trap. The government intervened, and when Haymour started acting irrationally and was charged with possessing a dangerous weapon, he had to be sent to a mental hospital for evaluation. It was a year before he could be released. While he was being treated an arsonist torched his home.

The government was able to purchase the island from him and partly restored it to its natural beauty. Following his release, Haymour returned to Lebanon where he ganged up with his brothers, conducted an armed raid on the Canadian embassy, took hostages and finally negotiated his return to Canada and a return to the courtroom. Seven years later he didn't get the island back but was awarded a small sum of money as compensation.

With the money, he purchased a rocky hillside south of Peachland, where he built an adult-themed hotel with heart-shaped tubs, garish red decor and love-nest suites.

Peachland Wine

Chateau Ste. Claire Estate Winery
5031 Cousins Rd., 767-2538.

First Estate Cellars
5101 Cousins Rd., 767-9526, 1-877-377-8788.

Greata Ranch Vineyards
697 Highway 97 S., 767-2768.

Hainle Vineyards Estate Winery
5355 Trepanier Bench Rd., 767-2525, 1-800-767-3109, www.hainle.com.

SUMMERLAND | POPULATION: 11,000

Sixteen kilometres (10 miles) north of Penticton, in the shadow of Giants Head Mountain (832 metres/2,600 feet), Summerland was the second community founded by John Moore Robinson. Originally on the lake, the town centre was moved west shortly after 1905 to a higher elevation, and from 1915 to 1964 it was an important stop on the Kettle Valley Railway. The lake-level part of the town is sometimes referred to as Lower Town, and a few kilometres south, where Trout Creek empties into the lake, is known as Trout Creek.

Summerland, in addition to several wineries, has two major tourist attractions: the Kettle Valley Steam Railway and the Ornamental Gardens.

Summerland's most famous citizen is undoubtedly playwright George Ryga who was born in the Ukraine and died in Summerland in 1987. In 1963, the year he moved to Summerland, he had his first public success with The Ecstasy of Rita Joe, the first English-language production put on at the National Arts Centre in Ottawa. By the mid-1970s he was recognized as one of Canada's leading playwrights and an outspoken social critic. He wrote 15 plays, five novels, poetry, short stories and more than 90 scripts for radio and television.

Summerland Attractions

DeLong Pottery
4420 Williams Ave., 494-5155, www.delongpottery. com.
Tucked away in a lush garden setting, the working studio of Anita DeLong features hand-built stoneware pieces individually decorated using motifs inspired by fruit orchards and vineyards.

Kettle Valley Steam Railway
18404 Bathville Rd., 1-877-494-8424, www.kettlevalleyrail.org.
Taking a ride on the KVR involves a pleasant 10-kilometre (6-mile) trip to the Prairie Valley Station, west of Summerland. It is well signed; just follow the arrows to the KVR. The 90-minute trip on the historic railway takes passengers through orchards, vineyards and typical Okanagan landscapes to the Trout Creek Bridge, the highest bridge on the original KVR. Don't worry, the heavy train doesn't go over the rickety old trestle, although a new surface with guardrails allows you to walk across. Passengers ride in an

Kettle Valley steam train

open cattle car or an enclosed passenger car while a 1924 Shay Number 3 steam locomotive does the pulling. A larger steam engine is being restored in a huge shed for future use. Throughout the year there are Murder Mystery rides, Great Train Robberies, BBQs and special events rides. Each ride has a musician, commentary and period costumes. There is a small museum at the station.

The Ryga House
5109 Caldwell St., 494-1666,
is the beautifully preserved heritage home of author George Ryga. The house serves as a retreat with rooms and facilities that can be rented.

Summerland Ornamental Gardens
4200 Highway 97, 494-6385, www.summerlandornamentalgardens.org.
The turnoff for the gardens, which are 2 kilometres (1.2 miles) up a steep hill, is opposite Sunoka Beach, 5 kilometres (3 miles) south of Summerland and 9 kilometres (6 miles) north of Penticton off Highway 97. Six hectares (15 acres) of trees, flowers and shrubs feature a hummingbird house, lush lawns, a walking trail to view the Trout Creek KVR Trestle, a xeriscape garden and exotic flowers everywhere you look. Picnic facilities and informative signs enhance the visit. Agriculture Canada

owns the land and buildings for this historic garden, while the Friends of the Garden Society is responsible for educating the public and promoting the gardens. Admission is free; a donation is requested. The orchards and big greenhouse that you pass on the way in are part of the Pacific Agri-Food Research Centre. Several varieties of Okanagan fruit have been developed here.

The 1913 Trout Creek Trestle, highest on the Kettle Valley Railway, can be seen and accessed from the Ornamental Gardens pathway.

Summerland Sweets
6206 Canyon View Dr., 1-800-577-1277, www. summerlandsweets.com.
At the candy factory you can view a short video and then enjoy complimentary samples of syrups poured over ice cream. The manufacture of jams, jellies and candies from Okanagan fruit can be viewed. A large store offers bargains on factory seconds and samples of the various sweets.

Trout Hatchery
13405 Lakeshore Dr., just off Highway 97, 494-0491.
Summerland Trout Hatchery is the oldest ongoing trout hatchery in the province, dating back to 1929. Four full-time employees help the rainbow trout and brook char to produce millions of offspring each year. These are distributed to lakes in the southern interior of B.C. The number of fishing licences sold, which funds the hatchery, declines each year. Open to the public with displays, a video and viewing of the 14 fish tanks.

Summerland Wine

Adora Estate Winery
6807 Highway 97, 404-4200.

Scherzinger Vineyards
7311 Fiske Rd., 494-8815, www.scherzinger. com.

Sumac Ridge Estate Winery
17403 Highway 97, 494-0451, www.sumac ridge.com.

Thornhaven Estates
6816 Andrew Ave., 494-7778, www.thorn haven.com.

PENTICTON | POPULATION: 42,600
Once known as the Peach City but equally suited to Beach City, this medium-size (by B.C. standards) metropolis is wonderfully situated between the south end of Okanagan Lake and the north end of Skaha Lake. It now introduces itself as either Wine Country, or Gateway to Wine Country, and sides with Oliver, the wine capital of Canada, in promoting the vineyard culture, also known as viticulture.

The city also uses the motto "a place to live forever," which is close to what the word Penticton means in the language of the Native people, Interior Salish. Another translation, frequently used, is Pen-tak-tin, "a place to stay."

If time is limited, try the following "Amuse, Cruise, Schmooze and Views" tour to get a synopsis of the city. When entering Penticton from the north you will cross a small bridge that passes over the Okanagan River Channel. This waterway was created by the city founders. It eliminated a lot of swamp, controlled flooding and made it possible to build the city of Penticton. After crossing the channel, immediately turn left until you reach Okanagan Lake and then go left until the channel prevents you from going any farther.

Amuse: You've reached the amuse part of the tour with the 30-year-old rose garden next to mini-putt and bumper boats. Less than a kilometre (.6 mile) downstream (south) is a place to launch an inflated raft or tube to ride the channel (see Coyote Cruises, page 71). The rose garden has many varieties of the bloomers and in the centre lies a sculptured sun dial with the prophetic inscription "The sun sets to rise again," which came true, metaphorically, when the dial was stolen and then found and returned to the garden.

Cruise: Now it's time to cruise the beach and admire the fine specimens of the opposite sex. The road along the beach frequently hosts car shows and other demonstrations and there is a good selection of restaurants with patios facing the lake.

Schmooze: Schmoozing starts at the casino in the big Lakeside Resort Hotel on the lakeshore and in the bars in the north end and along Lakeshore Dr. It can extend to the yacht club and the art gallery farther east.

Views: The views start after you continue past the art gallery. Opposite the yacht club you will find the esplanade trail that winds up a hillside to give the views. Somewhat farther along the road leading to Naramata is Munson Mountain, with the best viewing in town.

Penticton Culture and History

Art Gallery of the Southern Okanagan
199 Front St., 493-2928, www. galleries.bc.ca/agso.
Features exhibits by local and national artists plus displays provided by various schools. Behind the gallery are the Ikeda Japanese gardens and a statue by Fahcheong Chong depicting three life-size children playing on the rocks.

Fahcheong Chong statue

Penticton Museum

Books N' Things
238 Main St., 492-6661.
The biggest used bookstore in the Okanagan, and possibly in western Canada, has more titles than the owners can count, plus nearly 10,000 videos available for rent. The videos focus on international, obscure, cult and the generally hard to find while the books cover nearly every subject. Best place in town for the bibliophile and videophile.

Lloyd Gallery
598 Main St., 492-4484, www.lloydgallery.com.
The huge, multi-galleried store displays some of the Okanagan's best artists, as well as internationally known and famous Canadian painters, sculptors and print makers.

Penticton Museum (a.k.a. R.N. Atkinson Museum)
785 Main St., 490-2451 (attached to the library)
Excellent presentation of pioneer and First Nations artefacts, wildlife, railways and boating that date to Penticton's inception. Donation requested.

S.S. Sicamous Heritage Park
1099 Lakeshore Dr. W., 492-0403.
The *Sicamous*, the largest remaining steel-hulled sternwheeler in Canada, and the smaller ship, *S.S. Naramata*, which was constructed about the same time, are displayed as museums at the south end of Okanagan Lake. When enjoying the beautiful fittings of the 70-metre (228-foot) sternwheeler it is easy to understand why she attained the regal title, "The Queen of Okanagan Lake."

The 310-passenger *Sicamous* was prefabricated in Ontario, transported by the Canadian Pacific Railway to Okanagan Landing, north of Kelowna, and reassembled for her launch in 1914. With an interior of Australian mahogany and Burmese teak, she was several steps above the standards for freshwater passenger boats. There were 40 staterooms with electric lights and steam heat. A luxurious dining room accommodated up to 70 diners who were served sumptuous meals, on silver and fine china, by waiters in bow ties and white coats. Four comfortable salons were available for passengers and, as well, there were lighted writing desks on a balcony and a smoking and observation room. A crew of 38 served the passengers' needs.

Twin engines pushed her at an amazing speed of 31 kph (19 mph), and with the latest firefighting equipment, 20 watertight compartments, a steel hull and six lifeboats, she was considered safe, if not unsinkable. Her name, *Sicamous*, means shimmering water, and Sicamous Junction, north of Enderby, was considered the gateway to the Okanagan.

Every day she departed Penticton before 8 a.m. for a 250-kilometre (150-mile) round-trip to Okanagan Landing, with as many as 20 stops on the west side of the lake and 10 on the east. For many isolated communities it was an essential link to the outside world.

In 1937 she was permanently retired. The interior has been restored and turned into a museum display-ing nautical and pioneer history. There is a huge model railway that displays the convo-luted route through the mountains of the Kettle Valley rail line. Plays and musicals with themes relating to local history are per-formed on board.

S.S. Sicamous

Tumbleweed Gallery
101-207 Main St., 492-7701.
Art gallery.

Penticton Amusements and Attractions

Apex Mountain (see Skiing and Boarding, page 118)
After the snow season, the mountain reopens in early summer for biking and hik-ing. A chairlift takes walkers and bikers to the top of the mountain for the best of scenery and effortless descents.

Casabella Princess
709 Sunglo Dr., 492-4090, www.casabellaprincess.com.
This 48-passenger pontoon boat/sternwheeler provides afternoon and evening cruises of the lake.

Car racing
Penticton Speedway, 490-0420.
Stock car and hit to pass racing Saturday and Sunday on an oval track, 15 minutes east of Penticton.

Casino
Penticton Lakeside Resort, 21 Lakeshore Dr. W., 487-1280,
www.lake citycasinos.com.

Coyote Cruises
215 Riverside Rd., 292-2115.
Rentals of tubes and rafts to float down the channel to Skaha Lake, with a bus to bring you back. You can also launch your own raft here.

Family Fun Centre
Highway 97, south of the airport, 493-9125.
Indoor video and arcade games, outdoor driving track, batting cages, bumper boats.

Farmers' Market
100 block of Main St., on Saturday mornings from 8:30 to noon.
The season extends from May to October.

SUSAN WOOD

Skaha climbing

Mini golf at Loco Landing

75 Riverside Dr., 770-1896.

A beautifully landscaped 18-holer with trestles, waterfalls and bumper boats.

Action and Adventure Paintball

on Highway 97, just south of Penticton over looking Skaha Lake, 493-GOT-U, www.aapaint ball.net/start.htm.

Water World

225 Yorkton, 493-8121. Pools, hot tub, water slides and arcade.

Skaha Bluffs

Slightly south of Penticton and east of Skaha Lake lies one of the top 10 rock climbing areas in North America.

Not to be confused with El Capitan or Mount Logan, the multiple peaks of Skaha Bluffs get their reputation not from height, but from variety, from numbers, from the type of rock and from the guarantee of warm sunny weather, which is contrary to what mountains usually offer.

Climbing is well established at Skaha, with close to 11,000 climber-days per year. About half the climbs are sport routes and half are gear, and the great majority are single-pitch. That probably doesn't matter much unless you are a climber. Approximately 60 different crags and 600 routes are accessible from the main 8-kilometre (5-mile) Loop Trail. A long, steep set of stairs leads from the parking lot (on private land where a fee is charged) to the trail.

Skaha Bluffs has been approved by the Okanagan Land and Resource Management Plan as a Class A provincial park, but it may take several years for this to be implemented. In the meantime, it's worth the walk to explore the bluffs and watch the climbers. If you want to give it a try, there are sport shops in Penticton with climbing equipment and Russ Turner's Skaha Rock Adventures will teach you the ups and downs of climbing.

To reach the Bluffs, go south on Main St. to the end and turn left on Skaha Lake Rd. Follow it and turn left on Yorkton and then turn right on Valleyview Rd. and follow it to the parking area.

B&Bs in Penticton

The city has a fine assortment of motels, hotels and campgrounds, but two high-end bed and breakfasts stand out.

Riordan House

689 Winnipeg St., 493-5997,

A heaven and haven for collectors. Every shelf, wall and ledge is crowded with plates, pictures, knick-knacks, sculptures, vases, clocks and things both old and new that defy description.

Gibson Heritage House B&B
112 Eckhardt Ave. W., 492-2705,

Caters to those who want luxuriously decorated, spacious, two-room suites with lots of privacy. It offers guest rooms with a queen bed, a sitting room, separate bedroom and private ensuite.

Penticton Dining

Dream Café
74 Front St., 490-9012.

Colourful, airy and aromatic, with Gypsy flair, this two-storey eatery has falafels, tofu, hummus, couscous, Gypsy platters and Korean BBQ. Evening entertainment is not uncommon.

Granny Bogner's
302 Eckhardt Ave. W., 493-2711, www.grannybogners.com.

Named after the grandmother of the founder of the restaurant, Granny Bogner's is housed in a 1912 Tudor house that was converted to a restaurant in 1976. The best European cuisine is leisurely served in quiet, intimate surroundings.

Theos
687 Main St., 492-4019, www.eatsquid.com.

This restaurant's reputation has spread beyond the Valley more than any other eatery over the past 25 years. The owners are from Crete and the food is Greek and nothing but Greek. The building's design brilliantly gives the open, airy ambiance of a Mediterranean island, with flowering bougainvillea hanging from balconies. The feeling of intimacy contradicts the fact that it seats 300 and is often full in the summer. It has been named British Columbia's Restaurant of the Year.

Channel floating

Penticton Wine

Benchland Vineyards
170 Upper Bench Rd. S., 770-1733, www.bench land.ca.

Calliope Vintners
1-866-366-0100, 494-7213, www.calliope wines.com.

Hillside Estate Winery
1350 Naramata Rd., 493-6274, www.hillside estate.com.

La Frenz Winery
740 Naramata Rd., 492-6690, www.lafrenzwinery. bc.ca.

Poplar Grove Wine & Cheese
1060 Poplar Grove Rd., 492-4575, www. poplargrove.ca.

Spiller Estate Winery
475 Upper Bench Rd. N., 490-4162, www. spillerestates.com.

Pentâge Winery
4400 Lakeside Road. 493-4008, www.pentage.com

NARAMATA | POPULATION: 2,000

The melodic name originated during a séance when town founder John Moore Robinson supposedly heard the spirit of a Native chief intone the name of his wife, Nar-ra-mat-tah. This unincorporated community, governed by the Regional District of Okanagan-Similkameen, occupies but a hundred or so hectares (250 acres) of gentle, sloping land along the east shore of Okanagan Lake, about 16 kilometres (10 miles) northeast of Penticton. The village is flanked on the north and south by benchland and several stepped plateaus occupied by orchards, vineyards and meandering country roads.

Founded in 1907, Naramata is the third Okanagan townsite developed by Robinson, the other two being Peachland and Summerland. Good swimming and picnic spots can be found at either end of the community.

Coming from Penticton, as is most likely (although you can come from Kelowna by way of Chute Lake on a rough road that is destined to be improved), one of the first sights is Munson Mountain, between Penticton and Naramata. Although it is not really high enough to earn the title "mountain," it is on the edge of the lake and you can drive, walk or pedal most of the way up. The pavement stops before the summit, but the final walk provides awesome vistas of the lake and Penticton. You have probably noticed the big white letters that spell PENTICTON on the hillside, visible from Highway 97. A footpath leads to the letters.

Naramata Inn

Naramata Attractions

Claybank Farm Lavender
610 Boothe Rd., 496-5788, www.claybank farmlavender.com.
A self-guided tour weaves through rows of fragrant lavender. In July there is a lavender harvest festival and on Sundays, workshops teach the making of beribboned lavender wands. Samples of many lavender products, such as soap, lotion and scents, are available.

James Hibbert Pottery Studio
3015 Naramata Rd., 496-5150.
If you think pottery is just baked clay, this is the place to have a change of mind. Hibbert uses metals, smoke, cracks and assorted colouring mediums to cleverly create original works.

Naramata Heritage Inn
3625 First St., 496-6808, www.naramatainn.com.
The inn was built in 1908 by John Moore Robinson, who started the fruit industry in this region of the Valley. Over the years this building has functioned as a hotel, a private girls' school and, in the 1990s, the home of Robinson's grand-daughter.

Kettle Valley Rail trail

The inn was closed and slowly decomposing when it was purchased, carefully restored and brought back to life in the late 1990s. Very little was changed and the new owners went to great lengths to duplicate the original construction materials when wood and windowpanes had to be replaced. The original 17 guest rooms were amalgamated into 11 larger rooms. The rooms have original claw-foot bathtubs, antique furnishings and private balconies overlooking the grounds and the lake. The inn also has a dining room and bar.

Naramata Heritage Museum
Robinson at Second St., 496-5866.
Old photos and artefacts of early Naramata and surrounding areas are presented.

Naramata Dining
Naramata Heritage Inn: No big decisions here. Take a seat on the patio at the Naramata Inn or Hillside Estate Winery (see Penticton Wineries) and enjoy the ambiance and the good food. Cyclists descending the KVR welcome this big winery and its bistro. There are plans to put in showers to perk up weary bikers and hikers.

Naramata Wine

Elephant Island Orchard Wines
2730 Aikens Loop, 496-5522, www. elephantislandwine.com.

Kettle Valley Winery
2988 Hayman Rd., 496-5898.

Lake Breeze Vineyards
930 Sammet Rd., 496-5659, www.lakebreeze winery.ca.

Lang Vineyards
2493 Gammon Rd., 496-5987, www.langvineyards. com.

Nichol Vineyard
1285 Smethurst Rd., 496-5962, www.nicholvine yard.com.

Red Rooster Winery
910 Lower Debeck Rd., 496-4041, www.red roosterwinery.com.

Highway or Byway?
Penticton to Okanagan Falls, or Circle Skaha

The best way to circle a body of water, from a scenic point of view, is clockwise, so that you are on the inside lane, with the best view.

Skaha Lake hosts Penticton on its north shore and Okanagan Falls at the south end. It is the easiest of the Okanagan Lakes to circle, either by automobile or bicycle, as the round trip totals less than 33 kilometres (20 miles). The east side of the lake is a pleasant alternative to Highway 97 and there is no severe penalty in time or distance. Although this route is just the right distance for a bike ride, be advised that the bike lane on the east side is intermittent and in several places the road is wide enough for two cars and little else.

This is an absolutely can't-get-lost route. Follow Main St. or Highway 97 south in Penticton and turn left at Skaha Lake Rd., which, not surprisingly, runs along the shore of Skaha Lake. For the complete circle, just keep the water on your right until you get back to where you started.

After seven or so kilometres (four miles) you reach an area signed as the California Big Horn Sheep Habitat. There are plenty of hiking trails, and if you search the hillside you may catch sight of the elusive ungulates. The rams have massive curled horns. These sheep require a very specific habitat that combines a grassland area in proximity to cliffs that provide a safe retreat.

The small community of Okanagan Falls, 17 kilometres (10 miles) from the start, straddles the south end of Skaha Lake. If an ice cream cone, fudge or homemade chocolate tickles your fancy, follow Highway 97 less than one kilometre out of town towards Oliver and stop at Tickleberry's.

To return to Penticton, simply follow Highway 97 north, but first have a look around this interesting town. (See Okanagan Falls, page 77.)

Immediately after crossing the bridge, when heading north on Highway 97, the first road on the left leads to the provincial campground beside the river. Continuing on that road takes you to a winery and then south to Oliver by a scenic highland route that passes several mineral lakes. It's badly signed, there are several roads with similar names and the chances are good that you will get lost.

Continuing north along Highway 97, a turnout on the right reveals a nice vista and a sign explains the history of Penticton and the origin of the name of the city. Descend into Penticton, pass some places of amusement and you are back at the vast sandy beach on the north shore of Skaha Lake where you started.

KALEDEN | POPULATION: 1,250

On the west side of Skaha Lake, 13 kilometres (8 miles) south of Penticton, this picturesque settlement originated as a camping ground for passing fur brigades. In 1909 a townsite was established as the centre of an orchard area and a contest was held to name it. The winning entry combined kalos, Greek for beautiful, and Eden.

Speaking of beautiful, Kaleden has the prettiest tennis courts in the Valley, next to the lake, with wind protection. There is also a park, playground and beach, all open to the public.

OKANAGAN FALLS | POPULATION: 1,874

Situated at what used to be two waterfalls draining Skaha Lake into the Okanagan River, the town was originally called Dogtown, a reference to Skaha, a First Nations word for dog. The community was a trading and salmon fishing centre. In the 1890s the town was promoted as a settlers' paradise. The twin falls, which gave the spot its name, have been replaced by flood control dams.

Okanagan Falls Attractions

Heritage House, Museum and Thrift Shop

This may seem like an odd combination but there they are, right on Main St. (Highway 97) as it curves south to Oliver. The Basset House is particularly interesting since it was purchased out of the 1909 Eaton's Catalogue, brought to Oliver by rail, and then by paddlewheeler down Okanagan Lake, and transported by horse team to Okanagan Falls. It is outfitted with period furniture. The thrift shop is half log cabin. The museum, which looks like a residence, is directly behind.

Flea Market

A large semi-permanent collection of vendors sells under canopies on the north side of Highway 97 on weekends.

Kenyon Park

On the north side of Highway 97 behind the plaza and flea market, with a sandy beach on Skaha Lake, washrooms, concession, picnic tables and a pavilion.

Tickleberry's

1207 Main St., www.tickle berrys.com, and

Wurley's, www.wurleys. com,

Inside the same building, providing something of a landmark for those with a sweet tooth. The former claims "best ice cream in the Valley" and has 265 kinds of the cold delight.

Basset House

Wurley's Chocolate and Fudge Company creates 80 flavours of fudge and almost as many types of chocolate, in big vats on the premises. The building also hosts crafts and souvenirs.

Okanagan Falls Wine

Blasted Church
378 Parsons Rd., 497-1125, www. blastedchurch.com.

Blue Mountain Vineyard and Cellars
Allendale Rd., 497-8244, www. bluemountainwinery.com.

Hawthorn Mountain Vineyards
Green Lake Rd., 497-8267, www.hm vineyard.com.

Stag's Hollow Winery and Vineyard
2237 Sun Valley Way, 497-6162, www.stagshollowwinery.com.

Wild Goose Vineyards and Winery
2145 Sun Valley Way, 497-8919, www.wildgoosewinery.com.

Kenny McLean

Okanagan Falls' most famous citizen is rodeo rider Kenny McLean, who won his first buckle in 1956 and dominated North American bronc riding, calf roping, steer wrestling and team roping. He was Canadian saddle bronc champion five times, all-around Canadian champion four times, and also won in calf roping and steer wrestling. On the U.S. tour he was rookie of the year in 1961 and national bronc riding champion in 1964, 1968 and 1971. In 1962 he was world saddle bronc champion and he is the only Canadian to win the international points crown. His riding earned him an Order of Canada and a place in the B.C. Sports Hall of Fame. He died in July 2002, at age 63, competing at a senior pro rodeo.

OLIVER | POPULATION: 4,505

With a dozen wineries within a dozen kilometres (eight miles) of town, Oliver has wisely dubbed itself the "Wine Capital of Canada." To entrench itself in that position, local entrepreneurs have purchased the old downtown fire hall and turned it into the Wine Country Welcome Centre with tapas-style restaurant, a wine and gourmet food boutique, a wine tour and information centre, and a small wine museum. A row of cabana-style stores is being created to sell produce and arts and crafts. The wine station is a place where small-scale grape growers can bring their produce to be crushed and turned into wine and sold to visitors. In early October the Festival of the Grape features food, wine tasting, entertainment, a craft fair, an art auction and the grape stomp.

An interesting thing about Oliver is that it is outpacing southern neighbor Osoyoos in becoming a year-round retirement centre for owners of recreational vehicles. Sometimes older motorhomers and fifth-wheelers lose their enthusiasm for the annual trek to Arizona or California because of the expense of gas, the cost of health insurance or the lack of a travelling companion. The Bel Air Cedar Motel and RV Resort is typical of the four Oliver "campgrounds" that keep their stay-at-home clients busy during the winter. A calendar of events is printed and, in conjunction with the local seniors' centre, there is entertainment practically every day of the winter months. Nine holes of the Inkameep Desert Canyon golf course stay open for the winter and in 2003 only 2 rounds were missed because of snow. While January golf is not a shorts and T-shirt event, the average daily high temperature is at least above freezing.

Fur traders were the first outsiders to visit the Oliver area and then it was the lure of gold that brought new settlers. In the 1880s gold was found east of Oliver and Camp McKinney grew to include five hotels and numerous saloons. When better quality gold was found west of Oliver, the town of Fairview developed with a school, bank and government offices. In 1902 the lavish Fairview Hotel burned to the ground, and shortly thereafter the gold ran out. Today there is nothing but a weedy field and descriptive signage at the site just a few kilometres along Fairview Rd., off Highway 97, south of town.

Oliver began amazingly late, by world standards. It was established in 1921 by B.C. Premier "Honest" John Oliver, who planned it as a settlement area for veterans of World War I. An irrigation system was built and the desert became a lush and prosperous fruit-growing area. One of the most interesting buildings in town is the Oliver Hotel, on Highway 97, which was originally built near Vancouver in 1912. Nine years later it was dismantled and moved to Oliver. That meant the entire hotel (except for the balconies) was hauled by rail to Penticton, by barge down Skaha Lake and then by truck into Oliver.

Nearby lakes, such as Tuc el-Nuit, Gallagher and Vaseux, are popular for canoeing, fishing, windsurfing and other water sports, except for powerboating, because motors are prohibited.

Highway or Byway?
Wine Country Alternative
Picturesque Black Sage Rd. meanders through orchards and vineyards and passes a half-dozen wineries as it stretches between Oliver and north Osoyoos. Going south from Okanagan Falls, turn left at the Vincor winery on the east side of Highway 97, following the signs to Inkameep Golf Course. You're on Tuc-el-Nuit Dr. Keep on it until it ends near the hospital in Oliver next to the Osoyoos Indian Band store, office and gas station. Jog left (downtown Oliver is to the right) and turn right onto Black Sage Rd. (continuing to the left, before the jog, is the Osoyoos Band school). After passing Burrowing Owl Winery, Black Sage Rd. becomes Road 22 and passes the photogenic abandoned buildings of the Haynes Ranch, before curving west. It then crosses the Okanagan River (a good birding site) and leads back to Highway 97 just north of Osoyoos.

See the Oliver wine listing for the many vineyards on this route.

Oliver Hiking and Biking
Okanagan Riverside ride
Next to the trestles and tunnels of the KVR, this is the best family cycling route in the Valley. The mostly paved path, known formally as the International Bicycling and Hiking Society Trail, starts where Highway 97 crosses the Okanagan River 9 kilometres

Endangered Waterway

Two environmental groups have named the Okanagan River the third most endangered waterway in Canada. Wildcanada.net explains it this way: "Channelized, highly developed, drained and dammed, the natural flow of the Okanagan River has been reduced to a minuscule seven kilometres (4 miles) from its previous length of 314 kilometres (200 miles). The waters of the Okanagan's tributaries have been over-licensed to hydrate one of the leading fruit and wine industries in Canada, causing further reductions in flows. Dams and flood control measures have been built to accommodate increasing urban development, dramatically diminishing the salmon populations in the river by limiting their access to historical spawning and rearing grounds. Due to this loss of habitat, the Okanagan Valley claims 30% of the province's endangered species and 23 nationally threatened, endangered or vulnerable species."

The nation's most endangered river is the Petitcodiac in New Brunswick, where a causeway has clogged the tidal bore.

(6 miles) south of Okanagan Falls and about 5 kilometres (3 miles) north of Oliver. The linear parkway follows the river for 18.5 kilometres (11 miles) going through Oliver and passing close to several wineries. (See the Hiking and Biking section.)

Golden Mile Trail:
This 10-kilometre (6-mile) hike or bike trail begins at Tinhorn Creek Winery, on Tinhorn Creek Rd., where signs direct visitors to the start of the trail. The route includes a golf course, the historic Fairview townsite, abandoned mine shafts and an old stamp mill. Maps are available at tourist information or the winery. (See the Hiking and Biking section.)

Oliver Culture and Amusements

Dominion Radio Astrophysical Observatory
White Lake Rd., 493-7505, www.drao.nrc.ca.

This facility takes pictures of things you can't see — radio waves. It uses the waves emitted by stars and other heavenly bodies to map the universe. The site of the eight antennas is within a circle of mountains that keeps out man-made radio interference. The antennas are sensitive enough to pick up a cell phone located on Mars. There is a self-guided tour with taped information and a small room with displays. Visitors must walk in 500 metres (550 yards) from the road, since emissions from automobile ignition systems interfere with reception.

Largest Dominion Radio telescope

Going north from Oliver on Highway 97, turn left onto Secrest Rd., follow it uphill to Willowbrook Rd., take a right to Willowbrook community, then take the left road (White Lake Rd.) and follow it. To get there from Okanagan Falls, take Green Lake Rd. up the hill, past the winery, past Green Lake (a bright beautiful emerald green) and into Willowbrook. Follow Green Lake Rd. and it will turn into White Lake Rd. and lead to the observatory. The seven white synthesis telescopes and the big 26-metre (28-yard) telescope can be seen from far off. This is beautiful upland countryside and there is a route from Penticton to Oliver, but roads are badly signed (there are three White Lake roads) and direction signs are non-existent. Chances are, you will end up close to Keremeos.

Fairview Kiosk
An empty field is all that remains of the gold-mining town of Fairview. An informative kiosk explains the old townsite, just a few kilometres south of Oliver on Fairview Rd., off Highway 97.

Okanagan Gleaners' soup barrels

Gleaners

336 Ave. (#3 Rd.), 498-8859.

Were it not for the Okanagan Gleaners, a lot of perfectly good fruit and vegetables would end up in the town dump. Instead, industrious volunteers gather culls and rejects, such as peppers that are not perfectly proportioned, tomatoes that are not the right shade of red, apples that have a blemish and beans that are too twisty. They cut and dehydrate the vegetables and make a soup base that is shipped in barrels to the poor in underprivileged countries. They provide several million cups of soup per year. Vacationers with a day or an hour to spare can help out any morning from May to November, and there are camping spots for those who wish to stay and help for longer periods.

Sign on First Nations land near Oliver

Oliver and District Museum

9728 356th Ave., 498-4027.

If you visit the old Fairview townsite and wonder what happened to the buildings, you can find part of the answer at the museum, where the 1896 Fairview jail sits right beside the 1925 house that holds museum displays. The museum building was originally the Provincial Police building and became Oliver's first heritage building. A self-guided tour features relics from Oliver's past with an emphasis on the agricultural heritage. Admission by donation.

Tube ride

At the Oasis Service Station, 498-3508.

Seven kilometres (4 miles) north of town on the highway, inner tubes can be rented to float down the river, with pick-up and return to the start.

Oliver Dining

Best of India
36094 Highway 97, 498-0872.

If you stepped into a restaurant in the Punjab, the food at Best of India is exactly what would be served. Owned by an Indian family, the lunches and dinners can be ordered with a spiciness rating between 1 and 10. The decor is nothing you will rave about, but the food is wonderfully different. Make sure you order chapattis and try a dessert. The owner is educated in the medicinal properties of food, so tell him what ails you.

Cock & Bull Cappuccino Bar
34849 Highway 97, 498-6261.

Best place to start the day in Oliver. Fresh-ground coffees, chewy bagels, breakfasts and lunches.

Oliver Wine

Black Hills Estate Winery
30880 Black Sage Rd., 498-0666, www. blackhillswinery.com.

Burrowing Owl Vineyards
100 Burrowing Owl Place at Black Sage Rd., 498-0620, 1-877-498-0620, www.burrowingowlwine.com.

Carriage House Wines
32764 Black Sage Rd., 498-8818.

Domaine Combret Estate Winery
32057 Rd. 13, 498-6966, 1-866-837-7647, www.combretwine.com.

Fairview Cellars
13147 334th Ave., 498-2211.

Gehringer Brothers Estate Winery
Rd. 8, 498-3537, 1-800-784-6304.

Gersighel Wineberg
29690 Highway 97, 495-3319.

Golden Mile Cellars
13140 316A Ave. (Rd. 13), 498-8330.

Inniskillin Okanagan Vineyards
32074 123rd St. (Rd. 11), 498-6663, 1-800-498-6211, www.inniskillin.com.

Jackson Triggs Vintners
Okanagan Vineyards and Sawmill Creek Wine, 38691 97th St. N., 498-4981.

Silver Sage Winery
32032 87th St. (Rd. 9), 498-0310.

Tinhorn Creek Vineyards
32830 Tinhorn Creek Rd., 498-3743, 1-888-484-6467, www.tinhorn.com.

OSOYOOS | POPULATION: 6,300

Pronounced *O-sue-yoos* by locals and *O-soy-ohs* by others. Originally it was Soyoos, an Okanagan native name meaning "the narrows" or "the place where two lakes come together." This narrows is where a bridge is now located. The story goes that Judge Valentine Carmichael Haynes added the O in front to make Soyoos sound like an Irish name. Had a Scotsman been in charge, it might be McSoyoos. Judge Haynes was the first white child born in Osoyoos, in December 1875, and he went on to become a major landowner and cattleman. He celebrated his 87th birthday, his last, by driving 200 calves a distance of about 35 kilometres (20 miles).

Osoyoos has the distinction of being one of the few places in Canada where the northern border town is larger than the neighbouring one to the south in the U.S. About 4 kilometres (2.5 miles) north of the 49th parallel, Osoyoos inhabitants number 6,300, while Oroville, 6 kilometres (4 miles) south of the border, claims about 1,760.

Osoyoos also has the distinction of being the warmest city in Canada, although there are many ways of calculating mean and average temperatures. Let it simply be said that the average January temperature is just above freezing and the average July temperature is 29°C (84°F), with 249.8 millimetres (10 inches) of rain falling annually.

The Sonoran (or Sonora, or Great Basin) Desert edges up from Mexico in the rainshadow of the mountains and briefly pokes into the southern Okanagan. Small prickly cactus hug the ground to keep warm, greasewood (antelope brush) and bunchgrass grow here, and scorpions and western rattlesnakes spread their minor terror.

Osoyoos Lake makes a wonderful recreational destination, with four public, sandy beaches. The lake is deep in the centre, which means five varieties of fish can be caught — largemouth bass, trout, kokanee, perch and whitefish. There are three boat launches and several marinas for renting boats, skidoos or paddleboats.

The Osoyoos Indian Band of the Okanagan Tribe is commercially developing a large chunk of its desert holdings, while preserving an even larger portion. The land stretches from its headquarters in Oliver to the top eastern side of Osoyoos Lake. On the east side of town the Band has opened a year-round campground (Nk'Mip Resort), a winery and a desert interpretive centre. In the plans are a nine-hole golf course and a hotel.

Osoyoos Attractions

Anarchist Mountain
provides one of the best and most accessible viewpoints in the entire Okanagan. It is just east of Osoyoos where serpentine Highway 3

climbs out of the Valley and ascends like a snake going up a wall. It provides the pinnacle of panoramas, encompassing lake, town, vineyards and Haynes Point campground, which is virtually an island attached to shore by a thread of road. From the bridge on Highway 3, travel east and you will quickly start climbing. Two parking spots offer excellent panoramas. The first, at 9.2 kilometres (5.7 miles), looks out on Osoyoos, the "spit" and the U.S. border. The second viewpoint, a half kilometre farther along, affords a view of the pocket desert on the east side of Osoyoos Lake. It's one of the most photographed spots on the B.C. highway system.

Artwork at Nk'Mip Desert and Heritage Centre

The drive up Anarchist Mountain goes from desert cactus to mountain pines in minutes. The summit is 20 kilometres (12 miles) from town and rises from 277 metres elevation (910 feet) at lake level to 1,233 metres (4,045 feet) at the top. In winter, Osoyoos has little snow, and remains mild, while on top of Anarchist the fields are white and the air is crisp. The mountain's name provokes many stories, including one about a gang of anarchists hiding out on the mountain. Or perhaps it comes from someone's last name, or from a band of rustlers, or from a hermit. Most likely it's none of the above, but they are good guesses since no one knows for sure.

Desert Interpretive Centres

The opening of the **Nk'Mip Desert and Heritage Centre** (1000 Rancher Creek Rd., 495-7901, 1-888-495-8555, www.nkmipdesert.com), puts the small town in the strange position of having two desert interpretive centres within a short drive of each other. Although both involve walking through the sparse terrain, they are different enough that both can be enjoyed without much duplication.

The Osoyoos Band's version of the desert focusses on Native life and customs, and has several First Nations' dwellings beside the 2 kilometres (1.2 miles) of gravel trails on which visitors can tour the property. Displays show Native crafts, customs and foods. Also featured is the western rattlesnake, which can sometimes be seen basking in the summer sun. The Nk'Mip Centre has a program to study the rattlers, which can reach 1.5 metres (almost 5 feet), by implanting transmitters under the skin so they can be tracked. So far they have found that the serpents slither up to 1 kilometre (.6 mile) from their dens. There are usually some snakes on display at the "snake motel," where they are held for a few days after being picked up on or near the trails.

Desert Centre
146th Ave., just north of town (495-2470, 1-877-899-0897, www.desert.org)

The focus of the 25-hectare (66-acre) centre is the natural environment. Consider these figures presented by the Desert Centre: the local desert has 100 rare plants, 300 rare invertebrates and 30 to 50 percent of Canada's endangered and vulnerable vertebrates.

A guide conducts tours along a boardwalk with four information kiosks, and points out plants and animals that a visitor would not normally notice. Snakes (but rarely rattlesnakes), birds and rabbits are commonly seen from the boardwalk and along the way there are preserved specimens of the spadefoot toad, scorpion and bat pellets (vomit). The guides point out the cacti, native grasses and invasive flora. There are also displays inside a building, but the highlight is watching at least three varieties of hummingbird vie for food from feeders.

Osoyoos Art Gallery
8711 Main. St., 495-2800.

Paintings, pottery, carving, sculpture and eclectic collections are displayed and offered for sale at the building with the blue canopy in front. Other arts locations are the Art Barn on East Lakeshore Dr. and Modified Arts just off Main St. behind Chippers restaurant.

Osoyoos Desert Model Railroad
11611 115 St., Buena Vista Industrial Park, 495-6842, www.osoyoosrailroad.com.

The largest Marklin layout in North America covers the floor area of a large home. This is Osoyoos' newest attraction, opened in late 2003.

Osoyoos Museum
At the bottom of Main St., next to the lake, the museum is promoted as "The best small town museum in Canada," and features one of the finest displays from the archives of the B.C. Provincial Police.

Pioneer Walkway
Alongside Main St. (Highway 3), short, convenient and pretty. Just east of the small bridge over the lake, on the south side, is a flowered, lakeside walk that's ideal for an evening stroll. There are even washrooms at the east end. This is the narrow crossing point that earned Osoyoos its name.

Spotted Lake
On the south side of Highway 3, 8.3 kilometres (5.1 miles) west of Highway 97. It is said there is one green circle on Spotted Lake for every day of the year. The number seems reasonable. The small lake gets its name from the peculiar aquamarine circles that dot its surface. These are concentrations of magnesium sulphate (Epsom salts),

Hummingbird at Desert Centre feeder

calcium, sodium sulphates and other minerals. It has been described more than once as "the only one of its kind in North America."

The lake was a sacred site to the Natives who called it lilx'w (medicine) for its power to heal. The government has purchased much of the land around the lake to thwart some vague commercial plans of previous owners to package the water and mud and sell it as a health potion. The Osoyoos Indian Band now owns the property. The lake is presently separated from the road by a sagging wire fence, but it is worth stopping to have a look. It is in a small valley next to the road. It is the first of several mineral lakes west of Osoyoos, but the only one with circles on the surface.

Windmill Teahouse
5302 Main S., 495-7055.
With its tall vanes standing out against the sky, this has been an Osoyoos landmark since 1974. There is a 36-seat teahouse, gift shop, stone grinding flourmill and thrill rides.

Osoyoos Hiking and Biking

Haynes Point nature trail:
On the south side of 32nd Ave., just before the provincial camping area, a well-signed trail (that is part boardwalk) leads from the parking area. The 1.5-kilometre (1-mile) walk winds through grassland and a marsh. There are plenty of signs and a raised platform for viewing. The campground is the most solidly booked in the B.C. parks system, so don't expect to pitch your tent in the summer without a reservation.

Irrigation Canal
A 2.5-kilometre (1.5-mile) hike or bike trail starts at the end of 62nd Ave. north of Osoyoos Secondary School and follows an abandoned irrigation canal that was once vital to local agriculture. The route goes under Highway 97 and past Strawberry Creek to a viewpoint that overlooks Osoyoos Lake.

Mount Kobau Trail
There are two marked trails on the top of Mount Kobau that take hikers along alpine meadows. The 5-kilometre (3-mile) Testalinden Trail has views of the Similkameen Valley and pauses near Testalinden Lake. The longer Kobau Lookout Trail takes hikers to the forestry lookout, which has a commanding view of the Okanagan Valley. The summit is about 20 kilometres (12 miles) from Highway 3. The access road begins at the top of Richter Pass, 11 kilometres (7 miles) west of town.

Osoyoos Dining

Chalet Helvetia
8312 74th Ave., 495-6333.
Voted best European eatery in the South Okanagan.

Wildfire Grill
8526 Main St., 495-2215.
Good dinners, more formal than friendly, intimate, but don't sit too close to the noisy kitchen.

Osoyoos Wine

Nk'Mip Cellars
1400 Rancher Creek Rd., 495-2985, www.nkmipcellars.com.
North America's first aboriginal winery and the Okanagan's most southerly. There is a $5 charge for tours.

Nk'Mip Cellars

THE OKANOGAN VALLEY: SOUTH OF THE BORDER

All Okanogan, Washington phone numbers use the 509 area code.

Osoyoos Lake straddles the 49th parallel and reaches into the United States, where the residents of the town of Oroville are the last to take advantage of the clear warm waters of the Okanagan (which they spell Okanogan). The pleasant Lake Osoyoos State Park sits at the spot where the lake, for the last time, reverts to being a river.

Unfettered by man-made banks, dams and channels the river slowly meanders south, twisting and turning, widening occasionally to a large pond and narrowing to burbling rapids. Several times it runs beneath the highway.

As a recreational waterway, it is all but ignored. Neither canoe nor motorboat plies its waters and locals seem to prefer swimming pools to its natural waters. Although many bridges cross it, access is rare and the river is almost invisible. The occasional sign directs anglers to fishing spots. Highway 97 obediently accompanies the river, taking advantage of its valley.

After crossing the border (normally a simple procedure), the traveller immediately notices a change in the countryside. The vineyards vanish (competing with Napa Valley's production isn't so easy with no international duties) and orchards take their place. But the orchards are smaller and the Valley narrows, and will continue to narrow, as it wanders to its confluence with the cold waters of the Columbia River near Brewster, Washington.

The Okanogan River drops about 30 metres (100 feet) between Osoyoos and the Columbia and gets progressively bigger as various streams, including the Similkameen River, join it. But compared to the Columbia, it is just a drop in the ocean. As the Valley narrows it gets more arid, and by the time it ends, the terrain more closely resembles the middle of Arizona or Nevada (without the huge cacti) than the lush, irrigated Okanagan of British Columbia.

The Okanagan/Okanogan is one of the few places along the enormous Canada/U.S. border where the Canadian side is markedly more populous and more prosperous than its U.S. relative. The American countryside is far more serene and natural. Automobile traffic is light and easygoing, although bicycle and pedestrian traffic is almost non-existent. In a reversal of fortunes, the giant houses and strip-malls of the north are replaced here with dilapidated homes (some with attached junkyards), and the somewhat dreary and dusty towns lack energy and development.

Another change that the northern traveller notices is the abundance of Mexican food outlets. Mazatlan taco stands are in every town and Mexican food restaurants line the main streets. In this section of the book there will be no recommended restaurants. Let it suffice to say, "Eat Mexican"—it's either the real thing or the Tex-Mex variation, but always good.

TOP
Vernon's Polson Park (see page 38)

BOTTOM
Highway 97 (see page 19)

WYLIE PHOTOGRAPHY

TOP LEFT
Summerland Ornamental Gardens (see page 67)

TOP RIGHT
Pear blossoms

LEFT
Arrow-leaf balsamroot (see page 127)

BOTTOM LEFT
Lovely lavender (see pages 56 and 75)

BOTTOM RIGHT
On the Beach, by Geert Maas. Figures digitally placed on the sand (see page 49)

TOP
The Okanogan River (left) ends at
the Columbia River (see page 93)

BOTTOM
Okanagan Golf Club (see page 123)

TOP
Vernon's Ogopogo (left) meets
Kelowna Kin

LEFT
Osoyoos Lake Beach

TOP
Summerhill Pyramid Winery
(see page 100)

MIDDLE
The Dolphins Statue, Rhapsody
(see page 150)

BOTTOM
Boardwalk along Kelowna's
lakeshore

TOP
Evening stroll on Pioneer Walkway,
Osoyoos (see page 85)

BOTTOM
Sunset over North Okanagan

TOP
Mineral rings on Spotted Lake
(see page 85)

BOTTOM
Winter calm leaves leaves on
trees in February (see page 25)

TOP
Double rainbow appears as
Okanagan Mountain Fire of
2003 is extinguished by rain
(see page 13)

BOTTOM
S.S. Sicamous Paddlewheel
Museum (see page 71)

At the terminal town of Brewster, where the Okanogan River vanishes into the Columbia like a hose into a swimming pool, the Spanish influence reaches its apex. A visit to Brewster is far less expensive than a trip to such Mexican towns as Tijuana or Mazatlan and the culture, on the surface, seems much the same. Pastel-coloured, one-storey concrete buildings (not adobe) are the standard. The signs for businesses are half English and half Spanish and the vast majority of the population that plays in the parks and walks the streets appears to be of Latin origin. In the main city park beside the swimming pool I watched two football (soccer) teams play and the shouts from the sidelines and on the field were all in Spanish.

Sign Commemorates Hiram "Okanogan" Smith

There are open-air car repair garages, and laundry facilities under a roof held up by two walls, much the same as you would find in the hot countries south of Estados Unidos. If a trip to Mexico isn't in the forecast, a jaunt across the border to Brewster is not an unreasonable substitute.

OROVILLE | POPULATION: 1,500

The town is named for *oro*, Spanish for "gold," as some of the precious metal was found nearby, in the Similkameen River, in the 1860s.

On the east side of Highway 97, 245 kilometres (150 miles) south of Salmon Arm, B.C., just before Oroville, an historical marker tells the story of Hiram F. "Okanogan" Smith, who, "in the late 1850s" became the first Okanogan settler and ran a trading post. In 1857 he planted 1,200 apple trees that were brought in by snowshoe and packhorse from Hope, B.C. Eleven of his trees, on the east side of the lake, are said to still bear fruit.

In Oroville a sign on the outside wall of the visitor centre says that Smith planted the first apple orchard in 1865. This date difference cannot be explained by the centre host, but it is important because Father Pandosy is credited with being the first white settler when he built his mission in Kelowna in 1857. A visit to the Old Train Depot Museum should sort it out, but there the host says he has seen many variations on the date and records are not precise. He has a handout from the Historical Society that states that Smith settled near the foot of Lake Osoyoos in 1858. He says he "has done the math" based on various documents and his opinion is that the settlement occurred in 1860.

Train Depot Museum at Oroville

Oroville Attractions

McDonald Cabin,
915 14th St.

This small cabin was built in 1882 as a home for the McDonald family. It became one of the first U.S. customs offices in the area. Inside are customs and pioneer displays. Still under restoration. Hours are limited.

Train Depot Museum,
Janis-Oroville Rd., 476-2570.

Oroville's Great Northern Depot began serving the town in 1907. Part of the depot is devoted to railroad items and local history. Outside is a caboose from the Great Northern that was retired in 1987.

Gold Digger Cellars,
1205 Main St., 476-2736,

Featured are wines, tasting and gift shop. Tours of the vineyard can be arranged by calling 476-4887, ext. 19. This is a new winery in what is described as "Washington State's newest wine region."

The Pacific Northwest Trail
Passes through Oroville as it runs 1,100 miles (1,800 kilometres) from Glacier National Park in Montana to Cape Alava on the Pacific Ocean. Hiking, horseback riding and, for the most part, biking are all permitted.

MOLSON GHOST TOWN

It's a ghost town like a dream come true, with dilapidated wooden buildings to root through, old machinery rusting in the rain, faded pictures still hanging on the walls and enough signs and other clues to enable a visitor to put together a picture of a town that might have been. And it's accessible by paved road, just 15 minutes from Oroville, where you'll see the sign "Elevation 3,741 ft., population 35." The sign refers to the population of Molson's "New Town." The population of the original Molson is zero.

The only missing ingredients are tumbleweed, tall cacti and the bleached skulls of thirsty cattle.

The number of residents has declined somewhat from the high of 700 in 1927 when the town had two theatres, five churches, several pool halls, a number of beauty salons, a three-storey brick school, car dealerships that sold 125 cars each year, and a train station that was serviced by one freight train and two passenger trains every day. Molson was the focal point of a highland area severed by an international border that hardly anyone acknowledged.

The weathered, wooden buildings huddle together on a wide patch of weedy dirt. A cracked sign proclaims nothing more than "Old Molson." No security guards stop visitors from touching and feeling, and no turnstiles seek an admission charge. A bank, two homes, an assay office, a saloon and a tiny building with a barely readable sign, "Knob Hill Exchange," have their doors open and welcome wanderers.

The bank has a complete teller's cage with steel grating and beautiful woodwork, plus an assortment of rusting pumps and a huge, out-of-place printing press. The ramshackle assay office hosts scales, typewriters, old pictures and other artefacts. Two log cabins are partially restored, have some furnishings and provide a glimpse of what life was like just past the end of the 19th century.

In its heyday Molson was so prosperous that two rival forces vied for power and a New Molson, where the 35 inhabitants now live, was established to compete with the original. Strategically located between Old and New is the high school, which is now a museum (no admission fee — just a subtle request for a donation), and the former mercantile store. The school follows a standard Toronto design for a secondary school and the windows were actually shipped from that city.

Old Molson, Washington

The town has many more Canadian ties and, since the road from Oroville twists northward, New Molson is just steps from the international border.

The strongest tie is with the Molson family of Montreal. The story goes that John Molson, son of the founder of the Molson brewery, was something of a black sheep in the family and was given a weekly stipend just to keep away from the family business. As a remittance man he travelled west, ended up in the hills above Okanogan and, for reasons known only to him, started a town. Naturally, he named it after himself. As luck would have it, gold was discovered and the town prospered until 1926, when the vein ran out and both Old and New were abandoned.

The high school museum is staffed by enthusiastic volunteers who tell interesting stories about the rivalries between the towns, including the time when the inhabitants woke up to find the only bank had been moved from Old Molson to New Molson in the middle of the night.

The school museum houses an amazing collection of abandoned household items, such as radios, toasters, stoves, butter makers and dishes. It also has a re-created classroom, an authentic Molson barbershop and an original post office.

To get to Molson from Oroville, turn left (east) on Center St. Turn left on Cherry and then right on Chesaw Rd. There is one more left turn along the way, where a sign points to Molson. To return by a different route, continue along the road you took into Molson, pass the lake, and continue onto the gravel and past the sign that warns of a bad road (not bad at all). You are now on the old rail bed. Stop and read the information sign about the town of Sidley, now completely gone. Eventually the gravel road meets the paved road that you took from Oroville, so turn right.

The Tourist Information office in Oroville offers a map of a Highland Historic Loop Drive that shows Chesaw, another ghost town, as well as museums and historical displays in the area.

CONTINUING SOUTH

After Oroville, Highway 97 winds south, passing through the small and unremarkable towns of Ellisforde, Tonasket and Riverside before reaching Omak and its close neighbour Okanogan.

Omak is best known for the Omak Stampede and the Stampede is best known for the Suicide Race that has been held on the second weekend of August for more than 70 years. The Stampede is a carnival, rodeo, art show, parade and pow wow. In the Suicide Race, a horde of horses and riders race down a dirty cliff with a pretty good chance that some of them will literally bite the dust. Fortunately the landing is soft — in the river.

In the town of Okanogan, the **County Historical Museum and Fire Hall Museum, 1410 2nd Ave. N., 422-4272,** exhibits dioramas, models, photographs and displays pertaining to local history, including a replica of an Old West town in the early 1900s. The museum is adjacent to Legion Park.

The County Courthouse, at the junction of highways 20 and 97, has looked down on the town from a hillside since it was built in 1915.

A few more miles along, Highway 97 passes Malott and the 2-lane road abandons its constant companion, the Okanogan River, in favour of its new beau, the Columbia River, which it follows west to Brewster. Then the two of them curve south, side-by-side, rolling into the distance. Our journey ends at Brewster, described previously, (see page 89) and the best thing to do here is enjoy the Latin flavour, take a dip in the cold Columbia if you can bear it, eat some Mexican food, read the historical signs and then turn around and head north.

Highway or Byway?
Brewster to the Border

The return trip need not be a repeat of the trip south. In fact, there are beautiful roads ahead and the byways are much more interesting than the highway. Just northeast of Brewster, turn left off Highway 97 onto Old Okanogan Highway. Immediately you are back in orchards just above the valley and shortly thereafter the rolling countryside turns into picturesque farms and ranches.

On the right is a sign for Verestar, and following it will lead to an assortment of huge radio telescopes similar to the ones at the Dominion Radio Astrophysical Observatory (see Oliver, page 78). In fact, they too are located within a protective circle of mountains. The big difference is that the Dominion Observatory offers a self-guided tour and a display area, while Verestar offers a "No Trespassing" sign and a locked gate.

The Old Highway becomes #215, and at either Okanogan or Omak (Cherry St.) turn left at a sign for Conconully. Now you are entering hunting and fishing territory, with lodges and camps on the various lakes and rivers. In Conconully turn right at the only real intersection (and buy gas at the only pump if you forgot to fill up), where the sign points to "Loomis, 23 miles." The pavement shortly turns to dirt with a washboard surface that is wide enough for a car and a half. It stays that way for close to 20 kilometres (12 miles) as it clings to the side of a small but steep canyon. Okanogan National Forest comes up quickly with stately evergreens. This is the place to bring a canoe or kayak to enjoy the serene rivers and lakes.

The pavement resumes and Loomis looms ahead, but it passes as just a cluster of a few houses. Palmer Lake, nestled at the foot of mountains that retain a touch of snow in early July, is a turquoise gem that makes the rough road worthwhile. At either end is a beautiful sandy beach where the clear waters are warm and inviting in summer. There is also a cement boat launch, but it seems sinister to launch a powerful, polluting, putt-putt into this sacred environment.

Nighthawk comes next, and the billing is for a ghost town, but it is likely to disappoint if that is what you have in mind. Certainly there are a few abandoned buildings, but they don't look temptingly old and several inhabited dwellings are nearby. Better to go to Molson, an equal distance away on the other side of Highway 97 (see page 90).

Shortly ahead you will be met by the sometimes grumpy customs officials who are the ambassadors that visitors first meet on entering a country. After you are allowed to pass this outpost, which is only open from 9 a.m. to 5 p.m., the road ends just ahead and a right turn leads past Spotted Lake on the way back to Osoyoos.

OKANAGAN LITE:
Borderline Conversations

The Web is a wonderful place to get information.

Recently, just after I learned stovetop cold fusion at "Doitathome.com," I wondered: What are the biggest metropoli in Canada? I also wondered about the plural of metropolis.

The point is ... Toronto, Montreal, Vancouver and Ottawa (including Hull) are universally listed as the top four. Calgary and Edmonton flip-flop for the next spot and then it's Quebec City, Winnipeg, Kitchener and Hamilton.

I recommend this list be committed to memory. Border guards use it as a secret question to test you when you exit the U. S.

"What's your name and nationality?" demands the surly guard.

"Hi, I'm Jim and this is my wife, Lian, and we are Canadians just returning from a delightful vacation in Brewster. What's your name?"

"I'm Shirley. Do you have anything to declare other than your imbecilic attitude?"

"Ha, ha. You're pretty quick Shirley. Do we have to declare our suntans?"

"No, but you have to prove your nationality by showing picture ID and naming the 10 biggest cities in Canada by population. Now."

"First let me ask you something, Shirley. Big boats go out to sea with engines gulping fuel and they catch tuna and they cook it up and they put it in little tins and a distributor sells these and makes money, and then they put them on a truck and drive a thousand miles and put the tins on the supermarket shelf, and mark up the price, and you pay 79 cents. How is 79 cents possible Shirley, and, how much duty is included in that price?"

Shirley doesn't hesitate a second but spits back, "Name those cities. You've got 10 seconds if you want to see home again."

"Ten meek voices order confederation; every queen wants kind harmony," I say.

"Spread 'em and put your hands on top of the car."

"But it's a simple mnemonic. Surely you don't expect a rote recitation. Ten equals Toronto, meek represents Montreal, voices represents Vancouver etcetera. By the way that's a great scowl you've got Shirley. Do you work on it?"

"Every morning before breakfast. When I got my graduate degree in patrolling harbour districts — a PhD — I was top of the class in Scowl 341. It's the standard government scowl. Thanks for the compliment, you can go."

JUST NORTH OF THE OKANAGAN
Should one venture north of Armstrong on Highway 97A, (97 itself veers northeast towards Kamloops) and thus, geographically, out of the Okanagan, the rewards are the small town of Enderby and a larger settlement with the odd name of Salmon Arm.

SALMON ARM | POPULATION: 15,400
The town gets its name not from a fish with appendages, but rather because it lies at the head of the southern arm of Shuswap Lake on the flood plain of the Salmon River. Despite the abundance of surrounding water, Salmon Arm is not on a natural harbour or a recreational waterfront. The biggest freshwater dock in B.C. is needed to reach beyond the weeds and mudflats to give the houseboats and powerboats a place to dock.

Dock in Salmon Arm

Salmon Arm Attractions
A short walk on the long wharf is a must for tourists. Watching the houseboats come and go is always interesting and on many summer evenings there are musical performances at the small bandstand in the adjacent park. Adjoining trails that go in opposite directions along the lakeshore lead to excellent birdwatching areas (one with a shelter). The trail that goes eastward is longer and excellent for biking.

R. J. Haney Heritage Park
751 Highway 97B, beside the KOA campground, 832-5243,
A prime attraction in Salmon Arm. There is no admission charge to the collection of restored buildings representing an era just past the turn of the century. Set on 15 rolling hectares (40 acres) these buildings include a school, tearoom, gas station, blacksmith shop, candy store, museum, log cabin, fire hall and home. Dinner theatre is held here twice a week in summer.

McGuire Lake
Those who find that the short walk along the town's long dock has

inspired a desire for more bipedal locomotion can circle McGuire Lake (it's the one with the fountain that you see when coming into town from the southeast on Highway 97B). Ducks and turtles abound, and there are benches and picnic tables. The Rotary Trail continues from the lake, goes under Highway 97B and leads to a ravine holding Turner Creek. Cyclists and hikers can continue in this direction to the trails on Little Mountain.

Canoe Beach

This is where locals head to swim. Take the Trans-Canada Highway (#1) east towards Sicamous and when it curves sharply, go onto 50th St. and follow the signs. After walking through the tunnel that goes beneath the train tracks (trains are quite frequent), a huge public beach with trees, grass, sand, a concession, a boat launch and washrooms awaits.

Farmers' Market

Fresh produce is sold at the Farmers' Market held in the Piccadilly Mall parking lot, Tuesday and Friday, 8 a.m. to 12:30 p.m.

Salmon Arm Dining

Forster's Prime Rib House
in the Prestige Resort Hotel, 251 Harbour Front Dr., 833-1154.

In a town where a good view while you eat is the exception rather than the rule, Forster's is the exception. Whether on the patio or indoors you can watch the houseboats come and go, listen to the concerts in the park or just eye the comings and goings on the huge wharf.

Herb Garden Restaurant
111 Lake Shore Dr. N.E., 833-4983.

This gem is hidden downtown and comes temptingly close to being "gourmet dining," but at a fraction of the usual prices for fancy fare. The meals are all homemade and in summer the plates come festooned with herbs and flowers that the owner grows in her own garden. They are not only edible, but are also delicious.

Salmon Arm Wine

These are two of the most northern wineries in North America.

Larch Hills Winery
110 Timms Rd., 832-0155, www.larchhillswinery. bc.ca.

Recline Ridge Vineyards and Winery
2640 Skimikin Rd., 835-2212, www.recline-ridge.bc.ca.

ENDERBY | POPULATION: 2,818

The very English name of this village just north of Armstrong came about because a literary group became enthralled by a Jean Ingelow poem about rising waters: "The villagers were saved by the chiming of the church bells playing the tune, *The Brides of Enderby.*"

While the community claims the charming title "The Top of the Okanagan," it is, in fact, at the bottom of the Shuswap. (That's based on the assumption that north is top and south is bottom, which, of course, makes little sense considering we all live on an orbiting orb.)

Enderby Attractions

Enderby offers a pleasant walk along the Jim Watt Heritage Riverwalk that follows the Shuswap River for 1.4 kilometres (nearly a mile). This is a favourite place for locals to cool off by floating on the river on tubes between the park and the bridge.

The Enderby and District Museum, 838-7170 on the highway by the traffic lights, has a collection of photos illustrating the area's heritage.

The adventurous might want to climb the Enderby Cliffs (see Biking and Hiking, page 105).

Looking north from Kelowna

3 FEATURE PRESENTATiONS OF THE OKANAGAN

The primary attractions of the Okanagan have always been found in the great outdoors—skiing, golf, hiking, camping, cycling, swimming, boating, etc. However, one could easily argue that recent increases in the number of theatres, cinemas, galleries, restaurants and other indoor entertainments warrant a cultural vacation.

Such an argument would undoubtedly enlist the wineries to substantiate that point of view. On the other hand, one could count the wineries as outdoor attractions since the vines obviously enjoy fresh air and sunshine.

Many wineries incorporate a short walk through their vineyards in addition to restaurants, sampling rooms and tours of the fermenting and bottling areas. Read on and decide if the indoors or the outdoors is your prime sphere of interest.

WINE AND WINERIES

Grapes have been grown in the Okanagan since missionaries planted them to make sacramental wine in the mid-1800s. However, only recently has winemaking become a class act. Since 1926, when the first commercial vines were planted, this area has had the reputation of producing "plonk" and other gulping wines for the uninitiated. That changed when the labrusca and French hybrid varieties of vines were replaced with *vitis vinifera*, starting 25 years ago. When free trade with the U.S. was introduced in the 1980s it was obvious that those varieties couldn't compete, so they were pulled out and new varieties that the government had tested were planted. The grapes grown today are mostly French vinifera varieties like Chardonnay, Merlot and Pinot Noir, or German varietals, such as Riesling and Gewürztraminer.

There are close to 60 wineries in the Okanagan and the Valley has achieved world recognition for both wine and grapes. There are now about 2,100 hectares (5,200 acres) of premium wine grapes growing in B.C. and all but a few hundred are in the Okanagan. More are being planted every year. Rare are the valley viewpoints from which row upon row of lush green vines cannot be seen.

The greatest concentration is in the hot sunny south, with the

Icewine

For the production of icewine, grapes are intentionally left on the vine well into the winter months for later harvesting. The resulting freezing and thawing dehydrates the fruit and concentrates the sugars, acids and extracts, thereby intensifying the flavours.

Genuine icewine must follow VQA (Vintners Quality Alliance) regulations that prohibit the artificial freezing of grapes. To make approved icewine, the grapes must be picked by hand in their frozen state, ideally at temperatures of -10°C (15°F). Picking must sometimes be done at night to take advantage of the lower temperature.

The frozen grapes are pressed in the extreme cold and the water in the juice remains frozen as ice crystals, with only a few drops of sweet, concentrated juice obtained from each grape. This juice is fermented very slowly. The finished icewine is intensely sweet and flavourful. Yields can be as little as five percent of normal, making icewine expensive.

The Okanagan vintner always risks losing the icewine crop because the winter temperature may never get low enough for picking.

amount of acreage devoted to viticulture tapering off in the north. Oliver claims to be the Wine Capital of Canada, while its neighbour, Penticton, bills itself as the Gateway to Wine Country and Osoyoos is Desert Wine Country.

Celebrating the bacchanalian art in the Okanagan are wine museums, numerous wine festivals, plus tours and free sampling at nearly all of the major wineries. Serious wine tasters are advised to keep their winery visits to four per day so as not to become seriously inebriated through enthusiastic tasting. A day-trip to each of the southern, central and northern grape-growing areas should round out a three- or four-day stay.

There are several wineries that go on the must-see list and several more for the must-taste list.

Summerhill Pyramid Winery

It bills itself as "Canada's most visited winery and the largest certified organic vineyard." It has something for everyone. While the adults are amused with the tasting, the kids can play games in a small parkette, or they can bang the big brass gong on the porch until their parents make them stop. The view over the lake is spectacular, but that, in itself, is not unusual for an Okanagan winery. A short walk takes visitors through vines to a Native earth-house, to a restored log cabin, and to a pyramid styled after Egypt's Cheops. Wine is stored under the pyramid and apparently gains pyramid power. Summerhill, in Kelowna, is reached by taking Lakeshore Rd. (it starts off as Pandosy) south along the lakeshore and then continuing straight where it becomes Chute Lake Rd. The winery is on the right. Look for the giant bottle floating in the air.

Mission Hill Family Estate Winery

This is an architectural wonder built on a hilltop in Westbank. Recently constructed in the style of a Moorish castle, it features a 12-storey bell tower, with four bronze bells handcrafted in Annecy, France, by the Paccard Bell Foundry.

The flowered grounds, planted with 4,000 trees and shrubs, plus the Valley vistas, are worth the trip. Unlike many other wineries, Mission Hill levies a charge for samples and tours (the cost is deducted from a purchase). A grass amphitheatre hosts operatic and Shakespearian presentations and the view and ambiance alone make any theatrical presentation memorable. To get there from Kelowna, head to Westbank on Highway 97, turn left onto Boucherie Rd. at the lights and follow Boucherie approximately five kilometres (three miles), then turn right onto Mission Hill Rd. Follow the road to the very top.

Tinhorn Creek Vineyards

This third must-see is easily found at 32830 Tinhorn Creek Rd. just off Highway 97 near Oliver. A self-guided tour of the winery allows you to spend as much or as little time as you desire viewing the winemaking process, but the most interesting part is a small demonstration vineyard set up in front of the main building. Signs explain planting techniques, disease, harvesting, and, most interesting, the cost of starting a vineyard in the Okanagan.

Silver Sage Winery

Just off Black Sage Rd. (32032 - 87th St., Rd. 9), near Oliver, it offers some unique wines. One, called The Flame, a dessert wine with a hot pepper floating inside the bottle, has both a sweet and spicy taste. They make iced wines (not icewines) that combine fruit, which is frozen after being picked, with a Merlot or Pinot Blanc.

Elephant Island Orchard Wines

Located at 2730 Aikens Loop, in Naramata, about 12 kilometres (7 miles) east of Penticton, on the east side of Okanagan Lake, it prepares novel flavours from such fruit as apricots, blackcurrants, pears and apples. They make rich dessert wines. The apple icewines are made from Fuji apples. According to the winery, Fujis are the only apples that retain their flavour and texture and continue to hang on the trees, after repeated freezes and thaws, while waiting to be picked.

Grapes Galore

British Columbia has about 2,100 hectares (5,200 acres) of vineyards, of which 81 hectares (200 acres) are in the Fraser Valley and on Vancouver Island and 2,024 hectares (5,000 acres) are in the Okanagan and close vicinity.

An Okanagan winery averages four tonnes of grapes per acre. That's 4,000 kilograms (8,800 pounds) of grapes per acre for a total Okanagan grape production of 20 million kilograms (44 million pounds). With 454 grams, or a pound, of grapes being made up of about 137 grapes, that means six billion grapes are grown here—a grape for every person on Earth.

Demonstration vineyard at Tinhorn Creek

DINING AND ENTERTAINMENT AT WINERIES

Most of the larger wineries have a restaurant on the premises and, naturally, a lengthy wine list to complement the food. If your taste buds beg for burgers, beans and BLTs, you are not likely to find them at these sophisticated eateries. A few typical items from the spring menu of Sumac Ridge Estate Winery near Summerland: pan-seared halibut with herb risotto; fresh asparagus and olive oil roasted tomatoes; smoked chicken frittata from fresh eggs; goats' cheese, roast peppers and house smoked chicken served with sautéed spinach potato. For dessert? Chocolate profiterole drizzled with caramel and chocolate sauces.

Shakespeare, chamber music, comedy, Broadway, jazz, drama, barn dance, and barbershop are some of the entertainments offered up by wineries. The settings are frequently a natural amphitheatre that looks out on a perfect panorama with a setting sun casting a rainbow of hues upon mountain and lake. Wineries regularly offering performances are Cedar Creek, Grey Monk, Hillside, Mission Hill, Sumac Ridge and Tinhorn Creek.

OKANAGAN LITE:
Whining and Wining and Dining

I've been trying to develop a nose for wine as well as a sophisticated palate that can discern bleach from Don Peregrine. In double-blind tasting it's a toss-up as to which I choose, although the profound aftertaste of the former helps me with my selection.

I used to chill my wine with ice cubes that floated in a short-stemmed mug that I slurped from. Now that I've had a few lessons in wine tasting I swoosh it around the delicate wine glass, sniff it, splash it around in my mouth and then, with a gulp, it's down the hatch.

These tasting concepts are particularly difficult for me since my introduction to wine was my father's home-made *eau de rhubarb* that he made from stalks that grew wild and looked suspiciously like burdock. After mastering rhubarb wine that was also used for etching on steel, he progressed through dandelions and crab apples until finally he arrived at his cultural apex with grapes. And not your garden variety *vitis vinifera*, but the luscious Niagaras and Concords that gently drop from the stem in supermarkets and are sold in bulk for 39 cents a pound. My father buys dropped, squashed, misshapen, blemished and loose grapes and rolls them through a crusher that bears a resemblance to the wringer on a washing machine my mother once owned.

My first lesson in wine tasting came at Nk'Mip winery in Osoyoos, where I learned that chomping on a slice of lemon after imbibing wine cleanses the palate and gives subsequent wines a different taste. Sure enough, I no longer remembered the taste of the preceding wine and the following one now had a fresh, somewhat fruity, shall we say, lemony flavour.

My second lesson was to swoosh the wine around in a long-stemmed glass to give it some air, which it badly needed after being corked up in a bottle for 38.6 years.

The pursuit of wine excellence has taught me a lot of different terms such as oenology and viticulture, which sound nice but actually have no meaning. The words I really like, and use most often, are smashed, soused, wasted, zonked, plastered, pie-eyed, hammered and, of course, drunk. A parallel problem is the pronunciation of the wine labels. Gewürztraminer, Ehrenfelser, Tonguentwister, and Boozeindebottle don't exactly roll off the tongue. I do better handling the four-letter words—milk, coke, soda, beer.

Another onerous task is the ritual of sniffing the cork. "Excellent," is my normal response. "Very corky. I'll take a dozen, and while you're at it, can I have a glass of wine?"

I have quite a way to go.

Most Popular Wines Purchased in the Okanagan

- Merlot
- Pinot Gris
- Chardonnay
- Red Blends
- White Blends
- Pinot Noir
- Cabernet Merlot
- Gewürztraminer

WINE EVENTS

Spring Wine Festival

Running in early May, the festival is more than 10 years old. 861-6654, www.thewinefestivals.com. In 2003, 26,000 people attended 85 events and spent $500,000 on event tickets and wines at various wineries. The festival consists mostly of dining and tasting at wineries throughout the Okanagan. Events range from free samples and snacks at wineries to a $160 epicurean dinner at Mission Hill Family Estate Winery. Afternoon seminars on the art of making and tasting are held in Kelowna and there is a consumer festival at the Laurel Centre and Rotary Centre for the Arts. Masters of Food and Wine is also held at Kelowna's Rotary Centre, while Bacchanalia takes place at Penticton Lakeside Resort. www.owfs.com.

Spring Wine Festival Dates:
2005: May 5 to 8
2006: May 4 to 7
2007: May 3 to 6

Summer Wine Festival

This event comes in August and is held near Vernon. In its third year with tasting, eating and seminars at Silver Star Resort, www.owfs.com.

Summer Wine Festival Dates:
2005: August 4 to 6
2006: August 3 to 5
2007: August 9 to 11

Fall Wine Festival

For seven consecutive years this has been ranked as one of the *Top 100 Events* in North America by the American Bus Association. The Fall Wine Festival runs for 10 days leading up to the Thanksgiving weekend in October.

This is the big one, with more than 150 events. The majority of the events are dinners and open houses at the wineries, but usually the wineries add special events, such as tours of their vineyards and such things as a hike to a gold mine. There is chamber music, cheese tasting and making, a clambake, lobster dinner, and seminars on everything obliquely and directly related to wine. Events are located throughout the Valley.

Festival of the Grape arrives in Oliver in early October. This is more of a family activity than other wine-related events. Highlights are live entertainment, food from around the world, kids' crafts, pony rides, games, wine tasting and the Grape Stomp.

Fall Wine Festival Dates:
2004: October 1 to 10
2005: September 30 to October 9
2006: September 29 to October 8
2007: October 5 to 14

Winter Icewine Festival

This event features Okanagan icewines, which are showcased for four days in the third week of January at Sun Peaks Resort north of Kamloops, 1-800-807-3257, www.owfs.com.

Winter Icewine Festival Dates:
2005: January 20 to 23
2006: January 26 to 29
2007: January 25 to 28

BIKING AND HIKING, WALKING AND JOGGING

The Okanagan is more wilderness than anything else and there is nothing quite like a hike or a bike ride to get in touch with the untouched surroundings. Here are a variety of routes and terrains including urban, rural and wilderness. They are arranged from north to south.

Armstrong and Spallumcheen

These communities are known for their hiking and cycling because they have some of the biggest spreads of gently rolling land in the Okanagan.

Rose Swanson Mountain has a 90-minute round-trip, gentle trail suitable for hiking families. Otter Lake has trails that birdwatchers will love and Thomas Hayes Ecological Walking Trail is a one-hour circular walk in an area frequented by the great blue heron.

Road cyclists will enjoy a 22.5-kilometre (14-mile) loop that starts on Wood Ave., north of the Armstrong Fair Grounds, and proceeds along Highland Park Rd., Sleepy Hollow Rd., Lansdowne Rd., Hullcar Rd., Knob Hill Rd., Schubert Rd. and back to Wood Ave.

Enderby

This small community just north of Armstrong, offers a short, but pleasant family route from near the centre of town, for a few kilometres along the Shuswap River, on a paved path. Lots of signs explain the history of boats on the river, and mills that used the river.

Contrasting this is a climb up the famous Enderby Cliffs for a strenuous two or more hours. Two trails access these cliffs, both through private property: seek permission before hiking. Follow Brash-Allan Rd. to the end and take the driveway to the right. The trail starts at a gap in the white fence, marked with red ribbons. An alternate route follows McNabb Rd. almost to the end. Stop at the old, white barn to the right. The trail starts up the bank on the left side of the road. This route is less arduous. Contact the Enderby Chamber of Commerce, 838-6727, for details.

High Rim Trail

This trail runs 50 kilometres (31 miles) between Vernon and Kelowna. The footpath, on the rim of a high plateau overlooking lakes and rivers, has no facilities, so only the hardy should set out to cover the entire distance. Start at the Cosen's Bay Gate of Kalamalka Lake Provincial Park. Take the left path, parallelling the fence. Watch for a marked path to the left, crossing the lower valley, and then climb up a steep path to join the old road leading to the telecommunications tower on the hilltop. Take water and food. Best hiked in sections, from access points off mountain lakes east of Oyama, Winfield and Ellison.

Kalamalka Lake Provincial Park

Many pathways lead through unique bunchgrass landscapes, through open grasslands, along cliffs, and through moist cedar and fir forests. Other trails lead to Deep Lake. Attractive beaches throughout the park are great for swimming, and interpretive signs tell about flora and fauna. (See also page 38.)

Kelowna

Excellent maps of cycling routes in the city, and maps of the rugged trails of the South Slopes, ravaged by fire, are available for free (or close to it) at bike shops.

There are two main pleasure rides and three areas for more athletic mountain bikers in Kelowna, the streets of which are endowed, for the most part, with excellent cycling lanes. In fact it is among the top North American cities when the ratio of bike lanes to automobile lanes is considered.

Lakeshore and North

Running along the lakeshore, between the bridge and Paul's Tomb (far north end) are about seven kilometres (four miles) of bike and pedestrian lanes comprised of relatively flat dirt and pavement. The paved part of this path starts at the bridge, twists through City Park, and follows the ins and outs of the lake and ends either at Sunset Dr., or, if you follow the pathway beside Brandt's Creek and then jog right slightly, at Ellis St.

By far the most popular walking and cycling area in the city is the clearly marked section of this lakeshore path running parallel to Water St. Near the yacht club it becomes a divided byway with bikes, rollerblades and skateboards on one side and pedestrians on the other. Getting lost is close to impossible.

When you reach the Grand Hotel, take the path beside the hotel going towards the lake and zigzag across the gates atop the tiny lock that adjusts the water level so boats can move between the lake and the lagoon. This takes you out on a peninsula and a wide boardwalk curves beside the lake. This is as enjoyable a family ride as you are likely to find in any city.

To continue the ride north, simply follow the lake as far as you can and then cross Sunset Dr. and go under an Oriental-style gateway to a path beside Brandt's Creek. Jog right at the end and you will end up at Ellis St. If you turn left you will reach the foot of Knox Mountain. Go left at the stop sign towards the lake and follow Poplar Point Dr. along the shore. The road will

Sculptured great blue heron in Brandt's Creek

steeply ascend for a short distance. Turn left at the top and you will see a steel vehicle barrier on your right. Go around this and follow a well-kept trail to the Paul's Tomb area (a trail leads uphill to the mostly buried tomb) where there are picnic tables, swimming and a toilet. Fit enthusiasts can continue past this point on a trail that leads uphill to Clifton Rd. and the Glenmore Highlands, and even McKinley Landing, which can be accessed by continuing along the dirt track and more or less keeping the lake to your left. New housing planned for this area may soon prohibit taking the trails. Alternatively, ride to the north end of Clifton Rd. and continue steeply downhill through woodland trails to the settlement of McKinley Landing. The highlands above Clifton are also being developed, but there is still plenty of singletrack leading up and then down the other side to Glenmore Dr.

The Greenway

Another popular ride/walk is known locally as "the Greenway" and follows Mission Creek from the Mission Creek Regional Park at Springfield Rd. and Leckie Rd., almost to where it empties into Okanagan Lake. A trail continuing upstream from the Regional Park is under development. This will add 8 upstream kilometres (5 miles) through to the bottom of Gallagher's Canyon and will end at the meeting point of Mission Creek and KLO Creek near Layer Cake Mountain and Pinnacle Rock.

Slightly downhill (when you start at Springfield Rd.), the wide, seven-kilometre (four-mile) Greenway trail stops at Lakeshore Rd., but anyone wanting to reach the lake can continue on any of the side roads. The surface of the Greenway is hard-packed fine gravel and a mountain bike or road bike with good tires will suffice. Walkers, wheel chairs, dogs, cyclists, joggers, those with baby carriages and horses all enjoy the route.

South Slopes (also known as Crawford Estates)

For fitness rides, long hikes and horseback rides on marked trails this is a popular area. This region was hit hardest by the Okanagan Mountain Fire of 2003 and many of the 238 houses destroyed were located here. Much of the forest was also destroyed, but there are a few sections that were untouched.

Until firefighters, forestry workers and volunteers have completed their work here, it should be considered unsafe. Dead trees that lean precariously against others can topple at any time, and ash pits can cave in and cause serious injury. (Ash pits result when the roots of a tree burn underground and leave a large hollow with a thin covering of dirt.) The area will rebound with fresh grass and flowers and it remains to be seen how many of the trees will recover. New growth of flowers, mushrooms, shrubs and trees will keep the terrain changing for many years.

Most people arrive by car and park at the power station at the end of Stewart Rd. in the East Kelowna area. There are many, many square kilometres of riding and walking, most of which is either uphill or down. Bellevue Creek forms an impressive canyon here as it cascades towards the lake.

If you keep going up and don't wander too far to the left or right, it's hard, but not impossible, to get lost. If you keep climbing upwards you will reach the KVR by bike in three or four hours. On foot it takes a full day.

Bike shops in Okanagan cities offer group rides, for the physically fit and somewhat daring, in a number of wilderness areas several evenings of the week, and they are a good source for information on which trails are open and closed.

Knox Mountain

The area where most Kelowna bikers and hikers meet their first challenge is Knox Mountain. Just getting to the top is a triumph for the average cyclist. At the north end of Ellis St. a paved road leads almost to the top. At the end of the this road, follow the signs for the Apex peak and take the short dirt trail to a shelter with one of the best views of the lake and the city. A second, more challenging peak is next to the end of the pavement right behind the picnic area. The park is criss-crossed with trails so hikers can take any route that suits their ability.

For those who want to stay on the tarmac, a paved path leads right, off the Knox Mountain Rd., about three-quarters of the way up the mountain. This goes to Magic Estates, where both Magic Ave. and Rio Dr. S. lead to Clifton Rd. A right turn at Clifton goes steeply downhill to High Rd. A right at High, then a right on Gordon Dr. and a quick left on Clement Ave. will return you to Ellis St. for a nice vigorous round trip. One can also continue, from the picnic area on the parking lot loop at the top, north above the lake and come out at another part of Magic Estates and, again, Clifton Rd. Signs do not mark the routes.

A bit more than halfway up Knox Mountain Rd. is a dirt road with a steel barrier to the right. This leads to beautifully tranquil and wonderfully silent Cathleen Lake, an oasis that isn't even on most maps. A dirt trail surrounds it.

Glenmore Highlands

Mountain biking and hiking trails in the Glenmore Highlands are close to the city and easy to find. Go north on Spall Rd. (which becomes Glenmore Dr.) for about five kilometres (three miles) and pass the plaza on the right. Go left on Union Rd., start uphill and look for dirt paths. This paved road is the beginning of a huge development that will see many thousands of houses built in the Highlands. The paved road leads uphill to a viewpoint that reveals a valley and the mountainous wilderness within the city. It is possible to reach the top of these and come down the other side onto Clifton Rd. Or ride up Clifton Rd. S., and once the road stops going uphill, head right to the end of Rio Dr., onto a dirt trail, and go over the top to Glenmore Dr. No trails are marked and there are no maps, so you are pretty much on your own, but if you get your directions confused, you know that Glenmore Dr. is on one side and the lake on the other. Most of this is private land, but the public has used it for years. Development will likely change this.

KVR

Those three initials can send hikers, bikers and just plain walkers into paroxysms of ecstasy: Kettle Valley Railway. Imagine cool, deep, dark tunnels, 16 wooden trestles hundreds of feet above rollicking rivers, a hard-packed trail that seldom climbs or descends at more than three percent and postcard views of lake and valley 1,000 metres (3,300 feet) below.

The bad news is that the Okanagan Mountain fire of 2003 has temporarily rendered the most visited part of this heritage trail inoperative. Twelve trestles were completely burned or damaged to the degree that they are unsafe. The wooden parts of two steel trestles were also burned.

The good news is that replacing them is inevitable. A task force has set out a $15 million plan to rebuild the trestles. This would not be the first time the trestles have been rebuilt — the wooden beams, first put in place in 1910, had a life of between 10 and 30 years and were replaced accordingly.

The Myra Canyon Trestle Restoration Society would like to see the rebuild completed before the end of 2005. As soon as a trestle is completed, a team of volunteers would install decking and guard rails. One of the sad aspects of the fire is that much of the original transformation of the abandoned rail bed to a recreational route was done by volunteer labour. Every year the trail was enhanced with additions such as improved planking, guard rails on trestles and portable toilets at busy sections.

The KVR is a part of the Trans Canada Trail and is a designated heritage site that attracts tens of thousands of cyclists and hikers every year. As well as destroying the trestles and forests along the 12-kilometre (7-mile) Myra Canyon section (the most spectacular and most visited part of the rail trail), it has damaged the businesses of many companies that specialized in guided tours along the old rail bed.

Knowing the Terrain

The Kettle River runs approximately from Big White Mountain to Midway (near the border between Rock Creek and Greenwood on Highway 3) and then into the U.S. The West Kettle River flows beside Highway 33 past Beaverdell and joins the Kettle at Westbridge. There is a tiny settlement called Kettle Valley on Highway 3, between Rock Creek and Midway, and when the railway started from Midway it followed the Kettle Valley. Thus the name.

There'll be a Change in the Weather

As a newcomer to the Valley I was pleased to be invited to join Herb Isaac's annual 2-day bike ride from McCulloch Lake to Penticton along the Kettle Valley Rail Trail.

In early June it was hot in the Valley, so I set off with minimum overnight provisions to keep my load light. As we drove, with a trailer full of bikes, up into the mountains, the temperature dropped, and while we unloaded I was amazed that snow started to fall. I wasn't entirely naive about the affect of altitude on weather, but since it was a warm morning and we weren't going that far, I hadn't given it much thought.

As the snow swirled around my bare legs I stopped and

CONTINUES ON PAGE 110

pulled my pyjama bottoms over my shorts, put on a light jacket and continued. The trail was dotted with crater-size puddles and going through or around them left me thoroughly wet and muddy.

Snow soon covered the ground and I dragged a spare pair of socks over my red hands. Ice clung to my wet pyjama bottoms. Since I had no intention of turning around and going home, there was little choice. I put my head down and with visions of a hot cup of coffee in front of the fireplace at Chute Lake Lodge, I pedalled furiously to generate some heat. It was the best cup of coffee I have ever had. An hour later my properly clad companions arrived. The second day was sunny and warm, and as we descended into Penticton I was happy I had not overdressed. In future years we did the ride later in June.

MORAL: be prepared for any kind of weather at any time of year on the KVR, or on any other outing that involves a change in altitude.

Assuming that the burned trestles of the KVR will be restored, a description of one of the world's greatest hiking/biking trails follows.

The most difficult thing to understand about the Kettle Valley Railway route is why it exists at all. Why is an abandoned railway line twisting through and around isolated mountains and seeming to come from nowhere and go nowhere?

Look at a map of British Columbia and it is plain to see that the numerous mountain ranges run in a north-south direction and the lakes and rivers that fill them also generally flow north-south. There are a few exceptions, but the Okanagan and, to the east, the Kootenays, are not among them. The Canada/U.S. border, on the other hand, ignores geography and runs east-west. When British Columbia joined the fledgling Canada, a railway was promised and when it was built it had to follow whatever east-west valleys could be found. Thus the railway came to Kamloops and followed the Thompson/Fraser Valley to Vancouver. That left the southern cities of the Okanagan and other parts of the interior of B.C. somewhat isolated.

Gold was discovered in the Kootenays, near Nelson, about 350 kilometres (220 miles) east of the Okanagan by road, or 110 kilometres (68 miles) in a straight line. The mountains made it much easier for Americans to come up from the south and take the gold out of the country than for Canadians to even get to the gold.

This created a demand for a Coast to Kootenay rail line to change the situation and prevent gold from leaving the country.

Up to this point the story is quite simple, but then politicians became involved, awarding Canadians and Americans the right to build railroads here and there. As a result many rivalries sprung up, with branch lines going this way and that. Many of these lines were interrupted by the need to disembark and take a boat to connect to another line, or they required travel through the United States.

The plan for the KVR was to extend a line from Midway, where the CPR's tracks from the Kootenays and other eastern points ended, to Merritt and its branch line in the Nicola Valley connecting to the coast. Since crossing Okanagan Lake was out of the question (there was not even an automobile bridge) the route had to go to Penticton at the south end of the lake. The only barrier was mountains — plenty of them. As trains cannot climb hills, let alone mountains, the challenge was to find a route with a maximum grade of about three percent. To achieve this the train tracks twisted and turned 205 kilometres (134 miles) to get from Midway to Penticton, which is 80 kilometres

(50 miles) in a straight line. Anyone who has driven east on Highway 3 from Osoyoos and gone over Anarchist Mountain will appreciate how impossible it would have been to get a train through that route.

The man who would oversee the construction of the railway and direct its operations for more than 20 years was Andrew McCulloch. Indeed, his name has become synonymous with the Kettle Valley Railway, which was also called "McCulloch's Wonder."

Five thousand men were navvies on the KVR, and work on one of the strangest railways ever built was completed within five years. It went from Midway, zigzagged though the mountains and touched on Beaverdell and Camri, and then went south to Naramata and Penticton. After that it twisted up the west side of the lake to Summerland and then set off through mountainous terrain to Merritt and Hope. The full route was first travelled on September 14, 1916. Throngs of welcoming citizens lined the tracks in every town along the way — the Coast-to-Kootenay connection had become a reality.

The railway provided a faster and more efficient route for Okanagan fruit going to market, and it carried ore and lumber to the coast, but it was simply too expensive and difficult to run. Winter storms as well as avalanches of mud, snow and rock took their toll.

In January 1964, the final passenger run was made, and eight years later the Midway to Penticton section was shut down and eventually the tracks torn up. Today we can thank Andrew McCulloch for his wonderful engineering and one of the world's most exciting bicycling and hiking routes.

With a combination of volunteer labour and materials, plus government financing, it will recover from the fire and soon be operational again.

Several KVR tunnels offer cool dark passage to cyclists and hikers

Myra Canyon

Myra Canyon, with its two dark, damp tunnels and 18 trestles, has always been the place to go if you can only take in a short segment of the KVR. The old rail line clings to canyon walls as it works its way across the mountains. The best approach is to arrange for pick-up and drop-off or use the services of a professional tour company. This way you can take several days and cycle the 54 kilometres (34 miles) from Beaverdell to McCulloch, stay at McCulloch Lodge, ride 50 kilometres (31 miles) the next day to Chute Lake Lodge, stay there, and continue cycling, mostly downhill, about 45 kilometres (28 miles) to Penticton and a rendezvous.

Another, quicker way to sample the KVR is to simply follow the many signs in Penticton in the direction of Naramata. This will get you started going uphill and you will come to one short tunnel quite quickly. But after that it's a long uphill haul to Chute Lake and then to the Myra Canyon section.

Chute Lake Lodge

From Kelowna it is possible to get to the Myra Canyon section in relatively short order. From Harvey Ave. (Highway 97) go south on either Gordon Dr. or Pandosy St. for a couple of kilometres and then turn left onto KLO Rd. (Kelowna Land Orchardists) and keep on it as it becomes McCulloch Rd. McCulloch zigs and zags but keep on it and follow the occasional signs to Myra. Keep alert for June Springs Rd. and turn right. This gravel road becomes Little White Forest Service Rd. but is frequently called June Springs Forest Rd. Conditions change with the seasons and with the irregular maintenance, but it is guaranteed to be bumpy and dusty. After about five kilometres (three miles) you will reach the KVR, but signage comes and goes, so be alert, because you are not looking for a major intersection but just a path 2 or 3 metres (10 feet) wide. Turn right and the trestles are ahead.

Chute Lake

Getting to Chute Lake from Penticton is straightforward. Go towards Naramata and take the right fork just before the village. It is well marked. Go about 42 kilometres (26 miles) on a rough road that is being improved every year and is scheduled for pavement. From Kelowna go south on Pandosy St., which becomes Lakeshore Rd., and then becomes Chute Lake Rd. Follow Chute Lake Rd. and, on a curve where the power lines come down the hill, turn left onto a paved road. This is 13 kilometres (8 miles) from Highway 97. There is no road sign (it's Hedeman), but shortly after turning there should be a sign to Chute Lake. The pavement curves sharply and after a few kilometres turns to dirt/gravel. It's a steep, bumpy climb at first, but any car that isn't too low-slung should make it.

When you intersect the KVR, about 9 kilometres (5 miles) after making the turn off Chute Lake Rd., the KVR trail/road is relatively wide. There are a few forestry signs on the trees but not much else to indicate that you have reached the KVR. Turn right and go 12 kilometres (7 miles) along the actual old rail bed to the lake and lodge. Slow down when you pass cyclists and hikers so they don't have to taste too much of your dust.

Overnight on the KVR
Chute Lake Lodge

If you are looking for a good place to sleep, the lodge at Chute Lake may not be the best choice. Noise travels from room to room like an echo searching for a place to roost, and to say "goodnight" to your bed-mate is to say "goodnight" to guests in the other six second-storey rooms.

On the other hand, quiet normally prevails, since each of the compact, rustic rooms comes equipped with no phone, no television, no radio and no clock. Additionally there is no toilet or sink in the room or even down the hall, as there is no hall. A nocturnal need for bladder relief necessitates a walk along a balcony, down a spiral stairway and across a wooded lot that is likely to result in one being jarred fully awake by stumbling on a root or thumping one's head against a tree while searching for a bathhouse either around the corner or up a hill.

There are dozens of reasons not to stay at Chute Lake Lodge, a prime one being that it is close to an hour's difficult drive along a dusty, rocky road from Kelowna. Penticton is slightly closer.

The highland lake itself is mostly too cold for swimming, and it is restricted to motors too weak for water skiing. Some hardy trout do await the determined angler.

A good reason to stay might be that you are hiking or cycling the Kettle Valley Rail trail and, after pedaling 100 kilometres (62 miles), have no interest in TV, phone or radio and neither a steaming locomotive nor chatter from other rooms could keep you awake.

Eight log cabins scattered randomly behind the lodge provide alternative accommodation with more privacy and are devoid of most of the same luxuries as the rooms, although each has a wood-burning cook stove, and running cold water and one cabin even has a toilet. Unlike the rooms, the beds have no linen, so a sleeping bag is required. Next door to the lodge, a camping area hosts those who have brought tents or trailers.

The best reason to visit Chute Lake Lodge is a love of nostalgia, collectibles, antiques and railway lore. If anyone were to catalogue the items displayed and offered for sale the number would approach 10,000.

The large restaurant, with a menu limited to burgers and fries, is a museum showing dozens of lanterns, hundreds of glass insulators, scores of saw blades, and countless hammers, nails, bottles, antlers and harnesses.

Some have price tags; most do not. Some things are for sale and some are not. You won't know unless you ask.

The windowsills are weighted with irons, toasters, bottles, signs and devices whose function is open to conjecture. In the middle of the room some patched plastic couches, likely from the 1960s, face a huge wood-burning stove that is a delight in the cold weather that is not uncommon at 1,300 metres altitude (4,000 feet).

A coin will induce a jukebox to play old tunes, another coin-operated device polishes shoes, and on the hour a clock imitates the coming of a train with a whistle and chugging sounds.

Behind the lodge a barn with an open side and assorted overhangs and add-ons houses a mammoth array of ancient chainsaws, washing machines, butter churns, licence plates (dating back to 1913), outboard motors, tools, grinders and much, much more.

It is difficult to ascertain if the barn is a museum, as the sign says, or a store, as the occasional price tag indicates. A small room inside the barn has a locked door and everything in it, from snakeskins to tube radios, has a price.

Doreen Reed cooks up famous apple and rhubarb pies in the kitchen, while co-owner Gary Reed tends to the collectibles.

Glass insulators are what got him started 30 years ago and those led to canning jars, beer bottles and everything else.

The walls of his barn are all but invisible behind advertising signs for soft drinks, coffee, tea, motor oil and the luxuries of life of 50 and 100 years ago. Nothing is restored and a Chrysler Imperial from the 1950s sits on flat tires. Automobile-related signs dominate, with names like Studebaker, Packard, Dodge Brothers, B-A gas, Whippet, Imperial, and more. The collector mentality is attested to by weathered, wooden signs that represent the Lodge's past: cabins $3.00, picnic $.50, tenting $1.00, boats $2.00 per day. The same services are available today, but prices have changed.

Chute Lake Resort Museum

Penticton

The path beside the Okanagan River provides pleasant Penticton pedalling for families and casual cyclists. This is the river channel that tubers and rafters float down as it connects Okanagan Lake to Skaha Lake. Highway 97 crosses the channel as traffic enters Penticton and again, at the terminus at Skaha Lake, as the road leaves town, so the path and the channel are easy to find.

Oliver

Two excellent biking/hiking routes, one partly paved and one dirt, are offered by this southern settlement.

International Bicycling and Hiking Society Trail

The 18.4-kilometre (12-mile) International Bicycling and Hiking Society Trail meanders alongside the Okanagan River from the bridge just north of Oliver, where Highway 97 crosses the Okanagan River, almost to Osoyoos Lake. The trail comes within a five-minute pedal of nearly a half-dozen wineries and is just a few kilometres from another six. About half of its length is paved, the rest is hard-packed and it runs beside the river. The 10 kilometres of the trail that are paved are the closest to town.

The trail starts at McAlpine Bridge and ends near Osoyoos, but for those wanting shorter rides (the full round trip is 37 kilometres or 23 miles), the trail can be accessed from five small roads that cross the river. Each gives access to the trail, the most southerly being Road 22. If you need to park, the old CPR train station in town, next to the river, is a good spot.

Golden Mile Hiking Trail

This unimproved gravel trail for hiking and biking winds along the foothills of the west side of the Valley, next to orchards and vineyards. The trail itself is about 6.5 kilometres (4 miles), although an alternative return trip along Valley orchards can add another 3.5 kilometres (2 miles). Start at Tinhorn Creek Vineyards (Road 7, off Highway 97) and follow the directions along rural roads past cherry, apricot, peach, apple and pear orchards, and past Fairview Mountain Golf Course. You'll arrive at the heritage townsite of Fairview and the kiosk that provides historical information about the early days in the South Okanagan. The trail officially begins about a kilometre along Old Fairview Rd. from the old townsite. It turns south, crosses a small creek and opens up into grazing lands. Along this old two-track road are the remains of abandoned mine shafts. A sign marks a 200-metre (650-foot) detour to the ruins of a stamp mill. The last leg of the trip leads to the foothills behind the vineyards. The vista reveals all the vineyards along the Golden Mile. Osoyoos is visible in the south and Oliver to the north.

If you are still energetic, turn south to Gehringer Bros. and Hester Creek wineries; otherwise continue down the hillside to the vineyards, where nearly all of the varieties of grapes grown by Tinhorn Creek Vineyards are planted.

SKIING AND BOARDING

After the summer tourists head home and the tasting cups from the Fall Wine Festival are cleaned up, new adventurers invade the Valley—the skiers and the boarders. They head for the mountains that protect the lowlands from winds and precipitation and that provide the most cherished of Mother Nature's winter products—deep, fluffy, powdery snow.

During the busiest times there are 20,000 people living in Okanagan alpine villages and double that number using the lifts that whisk them to the peaks of the mountains.

The Okanagan offers five areas for downhilling and four that are exclusively for cross-country and snowshoeing. There is one major winter resort for each of the three main Okanagan cities, plus smaller areas for Westbank and Oliver. Additionally there is one in Washington State.

Sun Peaks, near Kamloops, is the most fully developed resort, with busy schedules both summer and winter. Because it is part of the winter tourist ski loop as well as being a summer destination and located near Salmon Arm, it is included here, although it is just beyond the Okanagan.

Downhill

Silver Star, near Vernon, and Big White, near Kelowna, are owned by the same company, and both are in the major leagues of North American winter resorts. Apex, west of Penticton, is a contender.

Favoured by many local skiers are Crystal Mountain, close to Westbank, and Mt. Baldy, a hill enjoyed by residents of Oliver and Osoyoos. Loup Loup services winter athletes in the American Okanogan.

The major winter resorts all offer numerous activities to augment the skiing and boarding. These include such activities as dogsled rides, tube parks, snowmobile rides, ice-skating, horse-drawn sleighs and snowshoeing.

As befits its name, Big White is the biggest, with the most accommodation and the most lifts, but in the summer Big White vanishes from the activities map while Apex and Silver Star keep moderately busy with hiking and biking. Sun Peaks adds swimming, tennis and golf to the summer mix.

Under ideal conditions the winter downhill season at the big resorts can run from late November to mid-April. When conditions are less than ideal, it is the opening day, rather than the closing, that is usually affected, with start-ups coming as late as mid-December. The resorts generally close when the slopes are still deep in snow but their customers are busy getting out their golf clubs, bikes and boats.

The following are the pertinent facts and figures for the downhill resorts.

Alpine Village at Big White

All Okanagan, B.C. phone numbers use the 250 area code.
All Okanogan, Washington numbers use the 509 area code.

Silver Star
22 kilometres (15 miles) northeast of Vernon, www.skisilverstar.com,
542-0224 or 1-800-663-4431.
Summit: 1,915 metres (6,280 feet)
Base: 1,155 metres (3,780 feet)
Village: 1,609 metres (5,280 feet)
Vertical drop: 760 metres (2,500 feet)
Longest run: 8 kilometres (5 miles)
Difficulty: Novice 20%, intermediate 50%, advanced 30%
Lifts: 1 6-pack express chair
     1 detachable quad chair
     1 fixed-grip quad chair
     2 double chairs
     2 T-bars
     2 magic carpets
     2 tube lifts
Lift capacity: 14,700 skiers/boarders per hour
Terrain: 1,100 hectares (2,725 acres)
Snowfall: 700 centimetres (23 feet) annually
Cross-country: 105 kilometres (65 miles) of core trails. 80 kilometres (50 miles) groomed and track set daily; 4 kilometres (2.5 miles) of lit track.

National Altitude Training Centre:
549-6722.
Located in Silver Star Village, NATC is a fitness centre, at 1,611 metres (5,300 feet) altitude, with showers, change rooms, waxing room, climbing wall and 180-seat auditorium.

Big White
75 kilometres (45 miles) southeast of Kelowna, www.bigwhite.com,
765-8888, 1-800-663-2772.
Summit: 2,319 metres (7,606 feet)
Village: 1,755 metres (5,760 feet)
Gem Lake base: 1,508 metres (4,950 feet)
Vertical drop: 777 metres (2,550 feet)
Longest run: 7.2 kilometres (4.5 miles)
Difficulty: Novice 18%, intermediate 56%, advanced 26%
Lifts: 1 8-passenger high speed gondola
     4 high speed quad chairs
     1 beginner quad chair
     1 triple chair
     2 double chairs

1 T-bar
1 magic carpet
1 beginners' handle tow
2 tube lifts
Lift capacity: 24,500 skiers per hour
Area: 1,022 hectares (2,565 acres)
Cross-country: 25 kilometres (15 miles) of trails
Snowfall: 750 centimetres (24.5 feet) annually
Accommodation: Canada's largest totally ski-in/ski-out resort village with overnight capacity of 1,400.

Apex

33 kilometres (20 miles) west of Penticton, 1-877-777-2739, 292-8222, www.apexresort.com.
Vertical drop: 650 metres (2,000 feet)
Lifts: 5, including one high-speed quad
Snowfall: 600 centimetres (19 feet) annually
Area: 450 hectares (1,112 acres)
Snowmaking: Okanagan's most extensive system
Difficulty: Novice 16%, intermediate 48%, advanced 36%
Number of trails: 67.

Crystal Mountain

15 kilometres northwest of Westbank, www.crystalresort. com, 768-5189.
Vertical drop: 212 metres (700 feet)
Lifts: 1 triple chair
1 double chair
1 T-bar
Season: Mid-December to March
Terrain: 20 runs, 70 hectares (160 acres). Five runs for night skiing.
Novice (4 runs), intermediate (7 runs) and advanced (7 runs).
Longest run: 1.6 kilometres (1 mile).

Mt. Baldy

35 kilometres east of Oliver, 498-4086, 1-866-ski-baldy (754-2253), www.skibaldy.com.
Vertical drop: 427 metres (1460 feet)
Lift: double chair
Season: Early December to early April
Terrain: 17 runs, 85 hectares (225 acres)
Difficulty: Novice 33%, intermediate 46%, advanced 21%
Average snowfall: 650 centimetres (21.5 feet).

Loup Loup Ski Bowl

In the Methow Valley, Washington, at the summit of Loup Loup Pass on Highway 20; 20 kilometres (12 miles) from Twisp, 30 kilometres (18 miles) from Okanogan, 40 kilometres (25 miles) from Omak; 826-2720, www.skitheloup.com.

Vertical drop: 378 metres (1,240 feet)

Base elevation: 1,231 metres (4,040 feet)

Lifts: 1 rope

   1 poma

   1 quad chair

Longest run: 3.2 kilometres (2 miles)

Terrain: 220 hectares (550 acres)

Snowfall: 381 centimetres (12.5 feet)

Season: Mid-December to end of March

Cross-country: 40 kilometres (25 miles) of non-groomed trails.

Snowshoe: 2-kilometre marked trail plus 40 kilometres (25 miles) shared with cross-country.

Sun Peaks

55 kilometres (34 miles) north of Kamloops, 578-5484, 1-800-807-3257, www.sunpeaksresort.com.

Vertical drop: 881 metres, (2,891 feet)

Lifts: 4 quad chairs

   1 triple chair

   5 surface lifts

Capacity: 9,000 people per hour

Terrain: 114 runs including 12 gladed areas

Longest run: 5 miles (8 kilometres)

Terrain: 1,400 hectares (3,400 acres)

Snowfall: 559 centimetres (18.3 feet) annually

Cross-country: 40 kilometres (25 miles) total. 20 kilometres (12 miles) groomed and trackset.

Cross-country Skiing and Snowshoeing

While the ski resorts offer an assortment of cross-country and snow-shoe trails, the best terrain — away from the crowds and the noise of the lifts — is found in flatter areas dedicated to the lovers of loppets. Each of these is close to a downhill area and is associated with an Okanagan city. The listings are from north to south.

Sovereign Lake

Adjacent to Silver Star, 22 kilometres (15 miles) northeast of Vernon, 490-8200, www.sovereignlake.com.

Located in Silver Star Provincial Park, the Sovereign Lake Nordic Centre has 50 kilometres (31 miles) of manicured trails, a full-service day lodge, ski school and rentals. Combined with the connected

Silver Star Ski Resort trail system, there are more than 90 kilometres (57 miles) of interconnected trails.

Nordic Cross-country

Seventy kilometres (45 miles) southeast of Kelowna near McCulloch Lake, 769-5158, www.silk.net/nordic.

The area has 65.5 kilometres (40 miles) of trails, 32 of which are available for snowshoes. Facilities include cabin, warming hut, lessons and scheduled events. Trails are open for members and non-members and are designated as novice, intermediate, advanced and singletrack.

Telemark Cross-country Ski Club

Twelve kilometres (eight miles) northwest of Westbank, just before Crystal Mountain downhill resort, www.telemarkx-c.com, 768-1494.

Terrain: 35 kilometres (22 miles) of groomed trails with 2.5 kilometres lit for night skiing. Varied terrain with groomed trails. Visitors welcome. Lessons, lodge and race program.

APEX MOUNTAIN RESORT

Fun on the slopes at Apex

Nickel Plate

39 kilometres (24 miles) west of Penticton, just past Apex Resort, www4.vip.net/nickelplate, 492-7595. Operated by Nickel Plate Cross Country Ski Club.

Terrain: 56 kilometres (33 miles) of groomed trails. Base elevation 1,864 metres, highest point 1,930 metres. Trails for all levels of skiers. Claims the longest ski season of any club in the Western Hemi-sphere — snow falls in November and remains until June. Cabin, rentals and races.

OKANAGAN LiTE:
Kicking Across the Country

The good news came from an elderly German gentleman in the parking lot of Vernon's Silver Star Ski Resort who told me that cycling was the only exercise that properly prepared one for cross-country skiing. I bike often, and furiously, and it was just what I needed to hear as I scraped mud, animal droppings and assorted flotsam from the thick coating of rubbery wax that clung to the bottom of my old skis. I try cross-country skiing once a year just to remind myself why I don't do it more often.

But now that I knew I had prepared properly, I burst with confidence.

In the Alpine village a dozen colourful tents were set up to display gleaming ski equipment and, to my surprise, the denizens of the tents were offering to loan said equipment to complete strangers to demonstrate its worthiness.

"Do you skate?" was the first question.

"Yes," I answered, recalling that I had seen a frozen pond on my way in.

"Great, we'll get you outfitted then."

"You've even got sticks?" I enquired.

"Yep, two of 'em."

"In case I break one?"

"I don't think that will happen."

"What about a puck?" The expression on his face told me something was dreadfully wrong. He gestured to a chair indicating that I should have a seat. The two back legs sank in the snow and I tumbled backwards.

Ten minutes later I knew that skate skiing involves pushing oneself along the snow in a motion akin to ice skating, while classic skiers move with skies parallel. I opted for skate equipment since I have used that technique to move along flat terrain when my downhill skiing took a turn for the worse.

Equipped with the best in boots, poles and skis, I pushed off like a pro and almost got out of sight before making a fool of myself.

Later that day I was getting into the swing of it, pushing with left and right and making good progress as long as the lay of the land and gravity were somewhat in my favour. The slightest indication of an incline brought me to a stop as if someone had laced the snow with peanut butter. Muscle pain set in at the same time. Cycling had prepared me for cross-country skiing the same way eating cheesecake prepares one for basketball.

My effortless technique and the glory of the day encouraged me to go farther. After an hour I made a U-turn and was disheartened to discover that my skating technique had reached perfection merely because I was going downhill. The skating style did not permit my going uphill any faster than an overweight, three-legged turtle, several of which, as I recall, passed me. To make the worst-case scenario even more dreadful, the loop I was on was being used by Lycra-clad professionals who left me spinning in the breeze as they whooshed past and paddled up hills that normally required ropes.

When I came to these hills I reverted to classic-style skiing, but the glide wax caused me to shuffle back and forth on the same spot, melting the snow. Apparently I needed a sticky kick wax. I would like to put forth my case for hybrid skiing — kick wax on skate skis — for those unable to do either.

GOLF IN THE VALLEY

Golf is a huge Okanagan industry, on a par (excuse the bad pun) with the other tourism magnets — skiing and wine. With more than 40 golf courses, ranging from championship 27–holers, to recreational par threes, the Okanagan is a premier golf destination. Throw in dozens of driving rangers and putting courses and you've arrived in an Eden of golfing greenery.

The Valley's varied landscape is incorporated into each course. Forests, mountains, orchards, water and desert-like dunes create beautiful scenery and challenging holes. Add perpetual summer sunshine and you have courses that call out to golfers throughout North America.

The clubbing season is longer than anywhere in Canada except the coast, and it usually runs from the beginning of March to the end of November. That's a nine-month season. A season shortened by bad weather (skiers call it good weather) runs from April through October. The two shoulder periods are times to take advantage of lower rates and fewer crowds.

Penticton golf

Golf 365 in Oliver

Dedicated golfers who are willing to brave the brisk January air can head to Oliver, where nine holes of the Inkameep Canyon Desert course remain open all year. Snowfall usually interferes with driving and putting only a few days each winter. While you won't find many players in shorts and shirt-sleeves, the greens are grassy and the par five is just as hard.

BEST OF THE BEST

Four Okanagan courses, listed alphabetically below, stand out for their beauty, difficulty, design and international reputations. Interestingly three of them (The Harvest is the exception) are within communities of houses, condos and hotels that cater to the fairway aficionado.

Gallagher's Canyon

Located in east Kelowna, it provides a major league course that is an interesting test of golf in a very scenic canyon locale. It starts with one of the most challenging first holes anywhere. Also at Gallagher's is the Pinnacle course, a nine-hole executive that accommodates golfers of all skill levels.

Main course yardage: 6,823
Championship rating/slope: 72.4/130

The Harvest

Also in east Kelowna, the Harvest rates high for aesthetics, with a sweeping view over the city and lake. The course, located in an old orchard, appears easy. The wide fairways allow for hooks and slices, but demand accurate shots to the pin and an accomplished short game. The Harvest expertly combines cuisine with chip shots—a dining room overlooks the course and the Valley. Finish your round in the evening and then dine in the clubhouse as the sun sets over the course.

Yardage: 7,104
Championship rating/slope: 73/126

Predator Ridge

Just south of Vernon, this is a course either loved or hated. The reaction may be related to golfing skills, as this is not a course for duffers or high handicappers and it is a favourite site for professional tournaments. For the nearly $100 greens fee, the better-than-average golfer can try to get a taste of what it takes to make par in the big time. Predator has 27 holes designed by famed course architect Les Furber.

Yardage: 7,156
Championship rating/slope: 75.4/137

Okanagan Golf Club

Previously known as Quail Ridge, this club just south of Winfield opposite the Kelowna airport, consists of two courses.

The Quail Course, also designed by Les Furber, is particularly scenic but in a less spectacular way than some Okanagan courses. Nestled among pines, lakes and streams, it is a world unto itself and golfers should particularly enjoy holes 12 through 17. Hilly terrain makes walking this course a good workout.

Yardage: 6,871
Championship rating/slope: 73/135

The Bear Course gets its name because it was designed by Jack "the bear" Nicklaus's company. It opened in 1999 and is sometimes called "the Teddy Bear," because of its supposed easiness. Most will find it a good challenge.

Yardage: 6,852
Championship rating/slope: 72/127

THE COURSES

North and Central Okanagan

Aspen Grove Golf Course
10303 Bottom Wood Lake Rd., Lake Country, 766-3933.

Gallagher's Canyon Golf and Country Club
4320 Gallagher's Dr. W., Kelowna, 861-4240, 1-800-446-5322.

Harvest Golf Club
2725 KLO Rd., Kelowna, 862-3103, 1-800-257-8577.

Hillview Golf Club
1101 14th Ave., Vernon, 549-4653.

Hyde Mountain
Mara Lake, 836-4653, 1-877-677-4653.

Kelowna Golf and Country Club
1297 Glenmore Dr., Kelowna, 763-2736.

Kelowna Springs Golf Club
480 Penno Rd., Kelowna, 765-4653.

Lakers Golf Club
Vernon, 260-1050.

McCulloch Orchard Greens Golf Club
2777 KLO Rd., Kelowna, 763-2447.

Michaelbrook Ranch Golf Course
1085 Lexington Dr., Kelowna, 763-7888.

Mission Creek Golf Club
1959 KLO Rd., Kelowna, 860-3210.

Okanagan Golf Club
3200 Via Centrale, Kelowna, 765-5955.

Peaks and Ponds Putting Course
480 Penno Rd., Kelowna, 765-7888.

Predator Ridge
361 Commonage Rd., Vernon, 542-3436.

Royal York Golf Club
Armstrong, 546-9700.

Salmon Arm Golf Club
Salmon Arm, 832-4727.

Shadow Ridge Golf Course
3770 Bulman Rd., Kelowna, 765-7777.

Shannon Lake Golf Course
2649 Shannon Lake Rd., Westbank, 768-4577.

Spallumcheen Golf and Country Club
Vernon, 545-5824.

Sunset Ranch Golf and Country Club
5101 Upper Booth Rd., Kelowna, 765-7700.

Vernon Golf and Country Club
800 Kalamalka Lake Rd., Vernon, 542-9126.

Vintage Hills Golf Course
3509 Carrington Rd., Westbank, 768-0080.

19 Greens Putt and Play
2050 Campbell St., Kelowna, 769-0213.

South Okanagan

Cherry Grove Golf and Country Club
Vincor St., Oliver, 498-2880.

Desert Springs Golf Club
4217 45th St., Osoyoos, 495-3110.

Fairview Mountain Golf Club
Oliver, 498-3521.

Inkameep Canyon Desert Golf
37041 71st St., Oliver, 1-800-656-5755.

Osoyoos Golf and Country Club
12300 Golf Course Dr., Osoyoos, 495-7003.

Penticton Golf and Country Club
600 Comox St., Penticton, 492-5626.

Pine Hills Golf and Country Club
3610 Pine Hills Dr., Penticton, 492-5731.

Pleasant Valley Par 3
Penticton Ave. E., Penticton, 492-6988.

Ponderosa Golf Club
4000 Ponderosa Pl., Peachland, 768-7839.

Riverside Golf
2360 Government St., Penticton, 492-5847.

Sage Mesa Golf Club
3415 Pine Hills Dr., Penticton, 492-8814.

St. Andrews-By-The-Lake
White Lake Rd., Kaleden, 497-5648.

Sumac Ridge Golf and Country Club
17333 Hwy. 97 N., Summerland, 494-3122.

Summerland Golf and Country Club
Canyonview Rd., Summerland, 494-9554.

Twin Lakes Golf Resort
Highway 3A, Kaleden, 497-5359.

OKANAGAN LITE:
The Little White Ball Goes in the Hole Below the Flag

It's about putting a white dimpled ball into a hole the size of the exit from a toilet.

These holes — 18 in all — are 150 to 500 yards away from where you hit the little ball. First you hit it with a big stick. After that you hit it with smaller sticks until it rolls into the hole. You count the number of times you do that. Not hitting a lot is a good thing. That is the game of golf.

More Okanagan real estate is devoted to putting and driving, hooking and looking, and slicing and dicing, than is devoted to playgrounds, gardens, skateboard parks, tennis courts, bike paths, water parks and tattoo parlours combined. If all the holes of all the Okanagan golf courses were placed end to end there would be a narrow swath of greenery running from Kamloops to Penticton with enough left over to sod the town of Osoyoos.

Politicians and business owners (all of whom golf) work behind the scenes to ensure there is a minimum of one golf hole per 500 population. I'm serious, count 'em.

Golf is an angst-inducing activity. That explains the plethora of putters, how-to videos, lessons and other paraphernalia — like jet-assisted clubs made of laminated extract of plutonium.

Recently I stood at the first tee of a commoner's course and a sign said the hole was a par four. It was designed to humiliate me. I was competing against Joe Par who plays every round perfectly. He never wages the mental battle to slow the back swing, keep eyes on the ball and concentrate on the other dozen factors that would send the little orb straight to a flag that fluttered so far away that it could only be located with a radio-telescope. Get anything wrong and I am physically and mentally disgraced and unfit to breed. In tennis, hockey, basketball and a hundred other games where there is a winner and a loser, and the latter is a weak, snivelling malcoordinate admired by none and eliminated from the breeding stock because the cheerleaders flock to the winner. (Golfers become schizophrenic by beating themselves.)

A more serious problem I have with golf is getting my money's worth, which is amazing considering the game was invented by a Scot. There's no incentive to improve, because the better I get the less I receive for my green fees.

When I'm on the links I'm paying about 35 cents each time I hit the ball. If I take some lessons and break 90, my cost is going to go up to 45 cents per stroke. If I get really good and start competing, it'll be over 50 cents per hit. Naturally I want to hit the ball more and get my cost below 30 cents. But when I do that I'm told that I'm not a very good golfer and I need lessons.

OKANAGAN WILDLIFE

The original Okanagan terrain is the third most endangered ecosystem in Canada after the Carolinian forest and the tall-grass prairie. It is also home to 58 percent of the threatened and endangered wildlife species in B.C. The Okanagan's vanishing dry shrub-grasslands support a tremendous variety of wildlife but are vulnerable to the changes brought about by man.

The Okanagan is home to about 100 distinct types of wildlife habitat because of the remarkable number of landforms and climates and proximity to the deserts of the western United States. This region's habitats host some of the most diverse, rare and unique assemblages of plant and animal species in B.C. and Canada.

A Short List of Interesting Species

Following is an alphabetical listing of some of the fascinating wildlife found in the Okanagan. Some are rare while others are common.

Arrow-leaf balsamroot

Arrow-leaf balsamroot (*Balsamorhiza sagittata*)

This yellow-headed member of the sunflower family reigns as the floral emblem of Kelowna. In April it quickly opens up and decorates the lower parts of dry, rocky hillsides and then it dries up and shrivels away in the summer sun. The entire plant is edible and the Okanagan First Nations pounded the small sunflower-like seeds into flour for baking. The leaves were smoked like tobacco, eaten raw or steamed. The taproots, after being roasted or steamed, were hung up to dry until needed. Then they were soaked overnight and cooked the next day. The long stem looks somewhat like the shaft of an arrow and the leaf looks like the head. The root has a balsam smell.

Avocet

The Okanagan is the only major habitat in B.C. for this bird, yet the American avocet lives in a local dump. Kelowna's Glenmore landfill is where the elegant, long-legged bird likes to spend its summers. (Take Spall Rd. from Highway 97 until it becomes Glenmore and follow the signs — the nicely landscaped dump is on the right.)

The birds were there first, and when the landfill was built on a slough 30 years ago, the birds held their ground. Avocets require small islands that provide barriers between nesting spots and predators.

The big bird is easy to spot with its extremely long upturned bill, long pale blue legs, and a pinkish head. The birds' ETA is the first two weeks in May and departure takes place in early September.

Unfortunately their B.C. home is starting to stink. Local naturalists and the dump operators are working to build the birds a new habitat so they will stick around while their old home is dried out and sanitized.

Bats

The Okanagan has the highest bat diversity in Canada, with 14 to 16 species. Several are rare and all of these nocturnal mammals are interesting. Especially fascinating are the spotted bat, which is found nowhere else in Canada, the rare pallid bat and the western red bat.

The large spotted bat has the body of a mouse, gigantic pink semi-transparent ears that stick out like a pair of satellite dishes, and two leathery wings about the size of a starling's with a spread of 35 centimetres (14 inches). It weighs in at 20 grams (less than 1 ounce) — about the same as three loonie coins. It is among the rarest bats in North America.

The fur on its back is black, with three large white spots that give it its name and make it easy to identify. The underside is entirely white with black underfur. The spotted bat's huge ears, about 4 centimetres across (1.5 inches), are held erect in flight and folded back over the upper back when at rest. Like all bats, the spotted has five claws on each hind foot and uses these to hang head-down when roosting. The claws also enable it to climb rock faces.

Like other bats, it uses echolocation to hunt down moths but, unlike other bats, the high-pitched "metallic clink" sounds that it makes can be heard by the human ear. The spotted bat roosts and hunts alone and travels 6 to 10 kilometres (4 to 6 miles) to favourite feeding places every day in the summer. It is a relatively slow flyer.

The pallid bat can be distinguished by its prominent ears and eyes and its short pale fur, which is light brown dorsally, and tending towards white on the underside. It produces a musky skunk-like odour from glands on the muzzle. No studies have determined the function of this odour. The pallid bat is an opportunistic feeder that gleans prey from the ground and the foliage of trees and shrubs. Occasionally it pursues insects in the air as it hunts slowly, close to the ground, with rhythmic dips and rises. Instead of echolocation, the desert-adapted bat relies on sounds made by its prey — often crickets and scorpions. It listens for their rustling sounds over large areas of sparse vegetation and can hear the footsteps of a scorpion. The pallid bat eats small prey while it is flying, and consumes larger items back at its night roost.

In cold weather, bats become torpid and their body temperature drops in conjunction with the environment. Some hibernate in the winter and others, like the Okanagan's western red bat, migrate south.

The fringed myotis bat is an Okanagan resident easily identified by the fringe of fur on its tail. There are nine types of myotis bats in British Columbia.

With its crevassed cliffs, insects hovering over water, and abundance of decaying pine trees, Okanagan Falls is a favourite area for bats. Dusk and dawn are the best observation times. See Wildlife Viewing section for locations.

Bears

Bears are the residents of the hills of the Okanagan, but unless you are hiking or biking in remote areas you are unlikely to have the pleasure of meeting them. I say pleasure because, for the most part, they are timid and harmless. There is no guarantee of that, however, and a mother with cubs can be dangerous if she perceives a threat to her offspring.

Sometimes, in midsummer, the highland food supply dries up and the bruins have little choice but to move lower, to where the scary human population congregates. That's when people get alarmed. This happened in various parts of the Okanagan in 1998 and conservation officers killed 150 bears. Normally about six bears are rendered harmless every year, but since growth patterns come in cycles, another bear invasion may occur.

The two types of bear found in the Okanagan are black bears (which are sometimes brown) and grizzly bears, which are bigger, browner, and have a hump at the shoulders.

Grizzlies are comparatively rare, with an average of just one per year making an appearance in the south Okanagan, although there were none reported in 2001. In April of 1999 a grizzly was shot in Naramata after raiding a chicken coop. Interestingly, an ear tag identified it as one caught the previous summer and relocated to a remote area 70 kilometres (43 miles) east. In 2002, a 180-kilogram (400-pound) male grizzly (which was described as "skinny") was shot east of Penticton as it dined on a freshly killed cow.

B.C. has a healthy and stable black bear population estimated at between 120,000 and 160,000: about one bear for every 7 square kilometres (2.7 square miles). Black bears are abundant throughout most of the province. B.C.'s grizzly bear population, estimated at 10,000 to 13,000, is classified as vulnerable.

Black Widow Spider

The dreaded western black widow, although one of the most poisonous spiders in the world, is extremely timid and will avoid a confrontation. The last death in North America, north of Mexico, was more than 10 years ago and not in the Okanagan. This large (the abdomen can be about the size of a finger tip), hairless spider is generally all black except for a red hourglass mark on the underside of the abdomen. The female spider hangs upside down in her web, waiting, so that her red hourglass mark serves as a warning signal to a predator that sees her as a snack. When small edible creatures become entangled in the web, the black widow injects them with its poison. It is very secretive, doesn't like the direct sun and hides under rocks during the day.

California Bighorn Sheep

The population of 600 resides on the hillsides on the east side of Skaha Lake near Penticton, as well as the Fintry area on the west side of Okanagan Lake. They move up and down the slopes, with the seasons and the weather, seeking greenery to munch on. The males have massive curved horns that allow them to bash heads in fights for rights to females, which have shorter, thinner horns.

Cougar

Felis concolor, mountain lion, puma, catamount, deer tiger, Indian devil — by any name the cougar is an imposing but evasive member of the community of Okanagan wildlife. Secretive habits and astounding predatory abilities — the cougar is capable of killing a large moose or elk — have resulted in a wealth of human misconceptions and fears.

The average adult male weighs 60 kilograms (125 pounds) and the female 45 kilograms (100 pounds), making this the largest cat native to British Columbia. There have been several cougar taken in B.C. weighing between 85 and 95 kilograms (190 and 210 pounds).

Kokanee

Kokanee is a form of freshwater sockeye salmon that never makes it to the ocean. The fact that there are freshwater salmon in Okanagan Lake indicates that salmon once travelled this far from the ocean. Kokanee salmon (*Oncorhynchus nerka kennerlyi*) belong to the same genus as sockeye salmon (*Oncorhynchus nerka*), but sockeye are anadramous, meaning they can live in both fresh and salt water and migrate to the ocean to grow to maturity. Many lakes and streams in B.C. support both kokanee and sockeye, and sometimes they spawn side by side. Kokanee (a Native word meaning red fish) arose from sockeye. After the last ice age, Columbia River sockeye migrated into the Okanagan. Kokanee evolved when access upstream into the Okanagan was blocked and they became landlocked.

The kokanee that live in Okanagan Lake have not been doing well in recent years. Although 7.2 million of the salmon are estimated to inhabit the lake, you would never know it because they are seldom seen and never caught (a fishing ban went into effect in 1995). The exceptions are when they inexplicably die en masse, and float near the surface and when they spawn in

Cougar vs. Goats

It is not often an Okanagan RCMP officer has to blast his 12-gauge shotgun to protect the public, but that's what happened on February 5, 2002, in Kelowna. The officer shot a cougar at a rural residence in east Kelowna, where it had killed two miniature goats. The big cat leaped into the fenced goats' pen to make the kills.

Mission Creek and other inlets.

In 2002 biologists estimated that 152,000 salmon spawned in streams or along the shore of the lake — one of the highest totals recorded in the last 15 years. This is still about half what it was in the 1980s, although it is more than double the 2000 count.

The restoration of spawning beds, the fishing ban and efforts to reduce the number of mysis shrimp in the lake are cited as reasons for the upward population movement of the fish that generally grow to about 1 kilogram (2.2 pounds) but have reached 4 kilos (8.8 pounds).

Okanagan Lake supports two types of kokanee — the stream spawners and the beach spawners. During their entire feeding life the two types mix in the lake. At sexual maturity, three years, they migrate to their specific area, spawn and die. Stream-spawners head for the 14 tributaries of the lake in early September and complete spawning by mid-October. Shore-spawners head for spawning beaches along the lake shoreline and spawn from mid-October to mid-November.

About six kilometres (four miles) north of Oliver, up to 50,000 sockeye salmon return from the ocean each September to spawn. The young that hatch spend a year in Osoyoos Lake before navigating the dams on the Columbia River and heading for the ocean.

Quail

The plump little bird running along the ground with the wattle dangling over its beak is the California quail, a small game bird found in western Canada only on southern Vancouver Island and the Okanagan, where it feeds on seeds and insects. *Callipepla californica* was introduced in the 1860s. The male is distinguished by a black and white head with a prominent curved plume. Body colour is grey-blue-brown with white slash marks. In fall, California quail gather in large coveys. They roost in trees and scatter widely when alarmed. They would as soon walk as fly and often two parents will herd a dozen chicks across a busy street. The quail likes to live near humans and doesn't desert them in the winter. On sunny winter days it will emerge from its ground nest to stretch its legs and wings.

Rattlesnake

The western rattlesnake (*Crotalus viridis*), also called the Pacific rattlesnake, is the only strongly poisonous snake in B.C., but its bite is not generally considered fatal. A half-dozen humans feel the rattler's fangs in the Okanagan each year, but recover. Rattlesnakes are not aggressive unless disturbed, and cannot

Threatened and Endangered Species of the Thompson-Okanagan

MAMMALS
Pallid Bat
(*Antrozous pallidus*)
Spotted Bat
(*Euderma maculatum*)
Badger
(*Taxidia taxus*)
Nuttail's Cottontail
(*Sylviagus nuttalli*)
Western Harvest Mouse
(*Reithrodontonys megalotis*)
White-tailed Jackrabbit
(*Lepus townsedii*)

BIRDS
Western Screech Owl
(*Otus kennicotti*)
Lewis's Woodpecker
(*Melanerpes lewis*)
Burrowing Owl
(*Athene cunicularia*)
Flammulated Owl
(*Otus flmmeolus*)
Peregrine Falcon
(*Falco peregrinus anatum*)
Grasshopper Sparrow
(*Ammodramus savannarum*)
Prairie Falcon
(*Falco mexicanus*)
Sage Thrasher
(*Oreoscoptes montanus*)
Yellow Breasted Chat
(*Icteria virens*)

CONT. ON PAGE 132

strike beyond their own length. The bitten area swells alarmingly and 48 hours of antivenin treatment in a hospital is the cure.

The serpent inhabits rocky outcrops below 1,000 metres (3,200 feet) elevation and after a winter of communal hibernation emerges to feed on rodents, shrews and, sometimes, small birds. Coloured from brown to olive-grey with large, dark-brown splotches along the back, it grows to a maximum of 1.5 metres (5 feet). The rattle, located at the tail, consists of a series of loosely interlocked horny segments designed to scare off intruders.

Scorpion

Hardly anything is known about the six species that inhabit the south Okanagan — in fact, three of these species have been discovered recently and have not even received official scientific names. Scorpions live in sandy, dry areas, hiding under stones or in shallow burrows during the day. They hunt crickets at night. The sting of the northern scorpion (*Paruroctonus boreus*), the most northern of all North American scorpions, is said to be no more painful than that of a wasp.

Shrimp

An ocean-style trawler regularly plies Okanagan Lake, netting tiny mysis shrimp, which are too small to interest humans but are an ingredient in pet fish food. The shrimp were introduced years ago to provide food for the diminishing kokanee, but later it was discovered that they competed for food. Recent modelling work using Okanagan Lake information suggests that mysis shrimp consume six times the zooplankton that kokanee eat.

Spadefoot Toad

The great basin spadefoot toad is a small, rather rotund amphibian, grey or olive green in colour. Adults are up to 7 centimetres long (3 inches). The limbs are short and stubby and the body rather plump — a spadefoot can look like a large pebble. Their most distinctive feature, and the source of the name, is the small, black "spade" on the first toe of each hind foot. This hardened tissue allows them to dig into loose soil for shelter. The spadefoot likes drier habitats than most amphibians and it needs loose soil to burrow for shelter on hot days. Spadefoots hibernate in snug burrows and emerge in warm weather to breed. During extremely hot and dry weather they retreat again to wait for more comfortable conditions. They are primarily nocturnal even when not hibernating.

WILDLIFE VIEWING AND NATURE PRESERVES

These areas, both primitive and developed, are where you can experience the Okanagan's natural environment and learn about the things that grow there. Many of the preserves are away from the roar of highways, the city lights that spoil a night sky and the visual flotsam and jetsam (signs, pop cans, etc.) that are the legacy of civilization. The listings are arranged alphabetically within the areas.

North Okanagan

Allan Brooks Nature Centre (Vernon)

The Allan Brooks Nature Centre provides a virtual tour of the North Okanagan from one side to the other in the Habitat Room. The Discovery Room offers hands-on experiences. Visitors can stroll the Grassland Trail, wander through the Naturescape Gardens, learn how to use native plants to landscape and attract wildlife, take in an interpretive program, or just enjoy the vista.
Viewing Highlights: Watch for yellow-bellied marmots from April through September. In summer watch for western kingbird and eastern kingbird. While hawk and owl species use this area year round, the winter months are best for red-tailed hawk, rough-legged hawk, gyrfalcon, prairie falcon, snowy owl and short-eared owl.
Directions: Located southwest of Vernon in the old Environment Canada weather station. From Highway 97, south of Vernon, turn onto 16th Ave., then left onto Mission Rd. Continue as the road becomes Commonage Rd. Turn onto Allan Brooks Way.

Ellison Provincial Park

On the northeastern shore of Okanagan Lake, Ellison Park includes 200 hectares (500 acres) of forested benchlands above a rocky shoreline of scenic headlands and sheltered coves.
Viewing Highlights: Columbian ground squirrels from April to September. Songbirds are most visible from late April to early June and in September. Look and listen for olive-sided flycatcher; western wood-pewee; Hammond's flycatcher; western and eastern kingbird; red-breasted, white-breasted and pygmy nuthatches; solitary, warbling and red-eyed vireos; warblers; western tanagers and evening grosbeaks.
Directions: From Highway 97, go west on 25th Ave. (downtown Vernon), through Okanagan Landing Rd. and follow the Ellison Park signs. Park is 16 kilometres (10 miles) from Vernon.

New National Park

A $65 million national park will be established in the south Okanagan before 2008. The park will stretch from Mount Kobau, near Osoyoos, north to Oliver and west to the Keremeos/ Nighthawk area. It will link with conservation areas near Vaseux Lake and Cathedral Provincial Park. The park is to be an example of the Interior dry plateau, which is unrepresented in the national parks system.

California Quail.

Jim Grant Island

Jim Grant Island

Originally known as Whisky Island, it was purchased with the assistance of the North Okanagan Naturalists Club and renamed after its member, Jim Grant.

Viewing Highlights: This small rocky outcrop is home to a colony of ring-billed gulls. Three other gull species are known to use the island — California gull, herring gull and Glaucous-winged gull. Viewing is best from May to September. It is reported that this gull colony came into existence shortly after the Kelowna City dump on Glenmore Rd. was established. The dump is about 17 kilometres (11 miles) by air from the island.

Directions: Located in Okanagan Lake between Vernon and Kelowna at Carr's Landing. There is good road access to areas near Carr's Landing that overlook the island.

Kalamalka Lake Provincial Park

Virtually at the door of the City of Vernon, this example of north Okanagan grassland is dotted with ponderosa pine and groves of Douglas fir. The spring wildflower show is spectacular. The park has an all-season appeal to those interested in its natural setting. The sloping, paved trail has signs that describe the flora and fauna. A variety of animals, birds, reptiles and plants reside in this mosaic of grassland communities. To date, 432 varieties of vascular plants (having ducts that carry sap or other fluids) have been identified in the park, a rare find in such a small area. Rattlesnakes inhabit the park.

Viewing Highlights: Western meadowlarks are easily visible from April to June and August to September. Golden eagles may be seen during spring and fall migrations. Watch for Lewis's woodpecker, Clark's nutcracker, black-billed magpie, white-breasted nuthatch, pygmy nuthatch and common poorwill. Yellow-bellied marmot colonies are found throughout the park. Mule deer and white-tailed deer are year-round residents.

Directions: Located 8 kilometres (5 miles) south of Vernon city centre, off Highway 6.

Swan Lake

This recognized birding hot spot is at the north end of Vernon, visible from Highway 97.

Viewing Highlights: During migration periods (April through May and

August through September) sharp-tailed sandpiper and lesser golden plover are spotted occasionally. Rarities include American avocet, black-necked stilt and black-crowned night heron. Common waterfowl species include green-winged, blue-winged and cinnamon teals; ruddy duck; Barrow's and common goldeneyes; bufflehead; Canada goose and American coot.

Directions: Just north of Vernon along the west side of Highway 97.

Central Okanagan
Bear Creek Provincial Park
Five kilometres (three miles) of spectacular, well-marked hiking trails follow a picturesque canyon carved into the bedrock by Bear Creek. The creek has formed a cottonwood-lined delta.

Viewing Highlights: Kokanee spawn from mid-September to mid-October when there is sufficient water depth. Watch for white-throated swifts from mid-May to mid-October.

Directions: From Highway 97, leave Kelowna, cross the floating bridge, travel 2 kilometres (1.2 miles) and turn right onto Westside Rd. Continue to the park where the camping area is on the right side of Westside Rd. and the trails on the left.

Kalamoir Regional Park
Good trails wind through this park, which has plenty of songbirds.

Viewing Highlights: Black-billed magpies are resident. Keep an eye out for western and eastern kingbirds; cedar waxwings; western wood pewees; red-breasted, white-breasted and pygmy nuthatches; warblers; sparrows; western meadowlarks; orioles; Nashville warblers and common nighthawks.

Directions: Located along the western shore of Okanagan Lake, south of the floating bridge, off Collens Hill Rd. in Westbank.

Knox Mountain Nature Park
Biking and hiking trails provide many recreational opportunities throughout this natural setting in north Kelowna.

Viewing Highlights: From April to September watch for yellow-bellied marmots, yellow-pine chipmunks and red squirrels. California quails reside in the park as do mule deer. A variety of songbirds may be viewed. Look for black-headed grosbeaks; western bluebirds; chestnut-backed chickadee; red-breasted, white-breasted and pygmy nuthatches; black-billed magpies; chipping and white-crowned sparrows; western meadowlarks; evening grosbeaks and white-throated swift.

Directions: Go to the end of Ellis St., which leads north from Highway 97, and there is a road most of the way up the mountain.

Birdwatching — the Perfect Jaunt

The Okanagan Valley has one of the greatest bird diversities in Canada. Let's meet some of these feathered flyers by taking the perfect birdwatching tour. We'll start in the central Okanagan at lake level. Among the rolling grasslands and woods we'll see mountain and western bluebirds, eastern and western kingbirds, Say's phoebes, western meadowlarks, vesper and savannah sparrows and lazuli buntings. Climb to the mixed ponderosa pine/Douglas fir level and check off Hammond's flycatchers, western tanagers, Townsend's warblers and mountain chickadees. Ascend to the boreal forest and there are boreal chickadees, three-toed woodpeckers, spruce grouse, pine grosbeaks, olive-sided flycatchers and rusty blackbirds.

Return to the Valley and visit alkaline lakes in the Kelowna area and find American avocets, Wilson's phalaropes, eared grebes and other ducks and shorebirds. Along Kelowna's Mission Creek Greenway there is a chance to see veerys, northern water thrushes, least flycatchers, pileated woodpeckers and red-eyed vireos.

CONTINUES ON PAGE 137

Maude-Roxby Wildlife Sanctuary

A Kelowna wetland habitat re-established in the 1980s and early 1990s and known locally as "the bird sanctuary."

Viewing Highlights: Many varieties of birds have been seen here. Among them are common tern, mourning dove, cedar waxwing, orange-crowned warbler, Townsend's warbler and white-crowned sparrow.

Directions: On the east side of Okanagan Lake just a few kilometres from Highway 97, at Abbott St. and Francis Ave. just past the hospital.

Mission Creek Linear Park

Dykes with trails run along both sides of Mission Creek.

Viewing Highlights: Black-billed magpies reside year round. The winter months are best for American dippers. In spring and summer look for California quail, woodpeckers, western wood-pewees, dusky flycatchers, ruby-crowned kinglets, Gray's catbirds, vireos and warblers.

Directions: Located along the lower reaches of Mission Creek in Kelowna. Lakeshore, Gordon, Casorso and KLO roads all cross it, and Springfield abuts it.

Shannon Lake Regional Park

This pretty local park has gentle walking trails.

Viewing Highlights: See waterfowl in the lake and great blue heron from May to August. A wide range of birds has been recorded here, including calliope and rufous hummingbirds; red-breasted, white-breasted and pygmy nuthatches; western and mountain bluebirds; western tanagers, sparrows and orioles.

Directions: Located about 3 kilometres (2 miles) north of Westbank. From Highway 97 in Westbank, turn north onto Old Okanagan Rd., eventually turning right onto Shannon Lake Rd. The park is on the right.

Woodhaven Nature Conservancy

Woodhaven is one of the Okanagan's smallest preserves. The perimeter trail is only 1.5 kilometres (1 mile). Since the entire area is fenced, it is a great place to take kids. They can run free and aren't likely to become lost. An excellent paper at the entrance explains the area's three microclimates, and there are numbered stops for identification of trees and other features.

Viewing Highlights: Red squirrels, California quail, black-billed magpies, hummingbirds, woodpeckers and swallows. Songbirds include Nashville warblers, western tanagers, Cassin's finches and evening grosbeaks.

Directions: In Kelowna take Gordon Dr. south from Highway 97. After 7 kilometres (4 miles) turn left on Raymer Rd. (ignore the previous Raymer to the right). Stick with Raymer as it zigzags through suburban streets for 2 kilometres (1.2 miles) until you reach the Woodhaven gates.

South Okanagan
Chopaka Border Area

This dry desert habitat is popular with birders and is especially interesting during spring migration. The land on both sides of the road is private, but there is ample stopping room.

Viewing Highlights: Common birds from May to July include long-billed curlew, mountain bluebirds, sage thrashers, brewer's sparrows, grasshopper sparrows and western meadowlarks. Early morning and evening are best. Also seen through August are California quail, American kestrels, mourning doves and common nighthawk.

Directions: From Highway 3 between Keremeos and Osoyoos, take Nighthawk Rd. towards the Chopaka border crossing. The viewing area stretches along Nighthawk Rd. from Highway 3 to the border, which is about 21 kilometres (13 miles) from the junction of highways 97 and 3.

Haynes Point Provincial Park

A pencil of land that juts into Osoyoos Lake. In the rain shadow of the Cascade Mountains and protected from winter storms by the Columbia Mountains, this is Canada's only desert area.

Viewing Highlights: Families of California quail are a common summer sight. From April through September view marsh wrens, eastern kingbirds, Gray's catbirds, cedar waxwings, yellow-headed blackbirds and orioles. The best viewing occurs when there are fewer visitors in the park (not July and August).

Directions: Located 2 kilometres (1.2 miles) south of Osoyoos, off Highway 97 on 32nd Ave.

Mount Kobau

A good site to stargaze, as it was originally destined for an observatory that was never built.

Viewing Highlights: Mule deer year round. From May to August watch for hermit thrush, Brewer's sparrow and vesper sparrow.

Directions: A gravel road leads up the mountain. Access is from Highway 3, about 10 kilometres (6 miles) east from Nighthawk Rd. (to the Chopaka border crossing), and about 11 kilometres (7 miles) from the junction of highways 97 and 3 in Osoyoos.

The South Okanagan provides a small semi-arid desert habitat with sagebrush flats, rocky cliffs and dry ponderosa pine forests. Not found anywhere else in Canada are black-chinned hummingbirds, Williamson's sapsuckers, canyon wrens, flammulated owls, white-throated swifts, white-headed woodpeckers and Gray's flycatchers.

One of the Valley's rarest residents, the sage thrasher, reaches the northern limit of its range at the Chopaka border crossing near Osoyoos.

North of Osoyoos, Road 22 has wetlands, sagebrush, riparian woods and open fields that are home to bobolinks, prairie falcons, lark sparrows, yellow-breasted chats, Caspian terns and American bitterns.

Vaseux Lake's cliffs host canyon and rock wrens, white-throated swifts, Lewis's woodpeckers and golden eagles. The woods near Vaseux Lake house Pacific-slope; and dusky, Gray's and Hammond's flycatchers. Also rewarding the birdwatcher are long-billed curlews, clay-coloured sparrows, common nighthawks, and possibly Gray's partridges and chukars. An owling trip may produce boreal, saw-whet, great horned, barred, long-eared, flammulated and western screech owls.

Okanagan Falls Provincial Park

Cool deciduous trees provide a contrast to the parched hills above. This oasis is famous among naturalists for its superb bird watching, wildlife viewing, nature study, photography opportunities and the variety of bats.

Viewing Highlights: This is one of the best sites in Canada to watch bats. A great variety of species have been recorded here and several interpretive signs provide information. The best bat viewing is in the evening, just before sunset, from the middle of May through July. Common birds observed in the Okanagan River are American dipper and fish-eating diving birds such as goldeneyes, buffleheads and mergansers.

Directions: Just north of Okanagan Falls, 500 metres ($1/3$ mile) south from the junction of Highway 97 and Green Lake Rd.

WYLIE PHOTOGRAPHY

South Okanagan birdwatching

Osoyoos Oxbows Fish and Wildlife Management Reserve

Dyke access along the Okanagan River, road access throughout, plus many trails provide visitors with opportunities to observe various habitats.

Viewing Highlights: An amazing list of wildlife species has been observed here. The area contains the reintroduction site of burrowing owls to the Okanagan and some may be observed on the eastern benchlands during the summer. Bird viewing is excellent in spring, summer and fall, especially during migration periods, when many rarities are spotted. Watch for long-billed curlew, bobolinks, California quail, black swifts, yellow-headed blackbirds, Gray's catbirds, canyon wren, common yellowthroats and lazuli buntings. In the summer months before dusk, watch for bats. In October kokanee spawn. Great basin spadefoot toads live in the area, as do Pacific rattlesnakes, western painted turtles and common garter snakes.

Directions: Along Highway 97 on the north end of Osoyoos Lake and along the Okanagan River. Access is via Road 22, about 7.5 kilometres (5 miles) north of Osoyoos.

Skaha Lake (East Side)

Bighorn sheep frequent the east side of Skaha Lake, close to Penticton.

Viewing Highlights: California bighorn sheep from October to March.

Directions: Take the only road along the east side of Skaha Lake between Penticton and Okanagan Falls. This area, near Penticton, is signed.

Vaseux Lake Wildlife Area

Viewing Highlights: During the summer enjoy families of ducks and geese. There are trails and some viewing structures. Sight canyon wren in spring and summer. From September to March watch for California bighorn sheep in the hillsides east of the parking area. Rattlesnakes are common. Trumpeter swan and tundra swan are sometimes seen in the north of the lake where the Okanagan River channel enters the lake.

Directions: On Highway 97 at the north end of Vaseux Lake, 5 kilometres (3 miles) south of Okanagan Falls.

White Lake Area

Another area that is popular with birders.

Viewing Highlights: Spring migration brings the wonderful and exotic sandhill cranes in mid-April. In May and June see sage thrashers, Brewer's sparrows, grasshopper sparrows and western meadowlarks in the sage habitat around the lake.

Directions: Access is from Highway 97 south of Oliver via Fairview White Lake Rd.

White Lake

FESTIVALS, FAIRS AND ANNUAL EVENTS

While the following agenda may appear impressive, it includes only annual events that have passed the test of time and have been held for several years. Many events come and go and some that are quite excellent do not continue for reasons that have nothing to do with their quality or popularity.

Races, exhibitions and celebrations at the mountain winter resorts are not included nor are commercial exhibitions or trade shows. Events in the American Okanogan are at the end of this listing, and Wine Festival events are in the Wine section (page 103).

Because dates and times change from year to year, only approximates are given. Websites and local tourist information centres can provide exact information.

OKANAGAN, B.C. CALENDAR OF EVENTS

The events are listed in chronological order.
All Okanagan, B.C. phone numbers use the 250 area code.

January
Polar Bear Dip
New Year's Day, Peachland, on the beach. Bring a bathing suit and towel. Sun block is optional. 767-2133.

New Year's Day Bird Count
South Okanagan Naturalists Club counts its feathered friends at Vaseux Lake. They spot thousands of individual birds in more than 100 species. The club also does annual counts in late December at other locations. Extra eyes are welcomed.
www.members.tripod.com/~sonc.

Kelowna Snowfest
Third week in January. Sno-pitch, water-skiing, wakeboard competition, outdoor volleyball, concerts, games, etc. Includes a polar bear dip in Okanagan Lake at Hot Sands Beach in City Park. Held for more that 30 years, sometimes without snow.
www.kelownasnowfest.com.

February
Bighorn Sheep Count
The South Okanagan Sportsmen's Annual Bighorn Sheep Count takes place on the east side of Skaha Lake near Penticton. A good time to see the sheep and to help count. 493-4055.

Vernon Winter Carnival
Parade

Vernon Winter Carnival
Traditionally starts on the first Friday in February and continues for 10 days. Hot Air Balloon Fiesta, ski races at Silver Star, ice sculptures, racquetball tournament, snow sculpture, snow pitch, Frisbee golf, music, food and night cross-country skiing lit by oil lamps. Biggest Okanagan parade is Saturday at noon, downtown. 545-2236, www.vernonwinter carnival.com.

Planned Dates:
2005: February 4 to 13
2006: February 3 to 12
2007: February 2 to 11
2008: February 1 to 10

Shuswap International Film Festival
Runs for five days in Salmon Arm near the end of the month. International films are shown at the Salmar Classic theatre. www.shuswapfilm.net.

Vernon International Film Festival
Held for three days at the end of the month. Sponsored by the Vernon Film Society with profits going to charity. Films shown are from the Toronto Film Festival circuit. Held at Vernon Town Cinema. www.vernonfilmsociety. bc.ca.

March
Okanagan Film Festival, Kelowna
Held for six nights starting the middle of the first week of March. In addition to screenings, there are workshops, competitions, classes, a reception and events for teens and for children. Paramount Theatre, www.okanaganfilmfestival.com.

Taste of Kelowna
Mid-March at the Grand Okanagan Hotel. A food-fest in which an admission fee allows customers to taste samples from some of Kelowna's many restaurants. It has been going for 16 years. 868-8447.

April
B.C. Interior Jazz Festival
Kelowna, early April. About 1,600 students compete in this festival that has been running for more than a quarter-century. There is a small charge for participant performances and adjudications. Also on the agenda is a gala awards ceremony and jazz masters' concert. 762-2049.

Boats-A-Float
Displays of boats and nautical equipment at the Kelowna Yacht Club on Water St., near the end of the month. 762-3310.

Kiwanis Music Festival
Performances in Kelowna and Penticton in March and for most of the month of April. Several thousand entrants compete in classical dance, speech arts, vocal, piano, strings, guitar and woodwinds. A 100-page program can be purchased for exact times and events. Open to the public and mostly free of charge. Showcase Concert requires paid admission. 860-5033 or 493-8322.

Multiple Sclerosis Super City Walk/Run
Starts at City Park, Kelowna, as well as Gyro Park, Penticton, in mid-month. Walk or run 5, 10 or 15 kilometres (3, 6 or 9 miles). 762-5850, 1-800-268-7582.

Fest of Ale: Penticton
Trade and Convention Centre, Friday and Saturday in mid-April. The organizers claim this is the biggest beer festival in Canada, with more than 25 breweries and microbreweries showcasing about 75 varieties of beer. Most are from B.C., but a few come from Washington State and Alberta. In addition to beer sampling, there is food and entertainment. Attendance is usually close to 6,000. 492-4355, 1-800-663-1900, www.fest-of-ale.bc.ca.

Ski to Sea
End of April, Kelowna. Teams and individuals race 97.5 kilometres (60 miles), from Big White ski resort to the lake at City Park, using six means of transport. The 700 competitors downhill ski, cross-country ski, mountain bike, run, road bike, and then canoe or kayak along the lake to the finish. Winning times are less than four hours. www.kelowna-ski-to-sea.com.

Horse Racing
Sonora Classic Endurance Ride, Summerland, end of April. Ride horses in an 80-kilometre (50-mile) cross-country event or 40-kilometre ride. Starts and finishes at Summerland rodeo grounds. 494-2686.

May
Garden Fair
Vernon, Polson Park, second weekend in May. Entertainment, kids' corner, face painting, games and lots of flowers. 542-1272.

Meadowlark Festival
Various sites in the south Okanagan over five days, encompassing the May long weekend. This series of nearly 80 events includes hikes, lectures, garden tours, bird watching, astronomy, biking, boating, gardening, horseback tours and nature photography. Typical of a Meadowlark Festival event is "Breakfast With the Birds, White Lake, 8:30 – 10:30 a.m. Enjoy a continental breakfast in a garden setting where ponds and bird-feeders attract a variety of forest birds, hummingbirds and woodpeckers. $15." There is also a nature expo at Okanagan University College, Penticton, and a banquet with a guest speaker. 492-5275, www.meadowlarkfestival.bc.ca.

Car Race
Knox Mountain Hillclimb, Kelowna, Saturday and Sunday of the long weekend. Billed as the longest paved hillclimb in North America and — at 50 years — the longest consecutively run motorcar event in Canada. Up to 90 cars race 3.5 kilometres (2.2 miles) up the twisty road to the top of Knox Mountain in Kelowna's north end. Also a car show, displays, a beer garden and food. 861-1515.

Horse Trials
Osoyoos, mid-May, Desert Park. More than 200 horses and riders participate in an international horse trials event with ditches, water jumps and fences. 446-2455.

Gold Panning
Cherryville. This unincorporated settlement 37 kilometres (23 miles) east of Vernon and just beyond the Okanagan, hosts the B.C. Open

Gold Panning Championships on the May long weekend. Everyone from families to professionals has a chance to pan for gold. Lessons, demonstrations and tours of an 1856 mine site. 503-1035.

Falkland Stampede
With close to 400 competing cowboys, this rodeo is the biggest event of the year for Falkland, population 620, a small community on the Salmon River, 45 kilometres (28 miles) northwest of Vernon. Close to $50,000 in prizes for the three-day, long weekend event with music, a parade and other festivities. The stampede has run for more than 85 years. 379-2627.

Maydays
Kelowna (Rutland), long weekend. A parade, games and displays in the park make up this vestige of a tribute to the birthday of Queen Victoria.

Walk to Cure Diabetes
A 5- or 10-kilometre walk (3 or 6 miles) starting on a Sunday, late May, at Jubilee Bowl in City Park, Kelowna. 1-877-287-3533.

Bike Ride, Okanagan-Shuswap Century
At end of May in the Armstrong-Salmon Arm areas. The Central Okanagan Bicycle Rider's Association organizes this annual back-roads tour covering 14, 56 or 100 kilometres (9, 36, or 62 miles) starting at Memorial Park in Armstrong. A bike ride of 100 kilometres or 100 miles is called a "century." 769-7108, www.oscr.ca.

World of Wheels Classic and Antique Car, Truck and Boat Show
Peachland. Sunday at the end of May. Several hundred entries. 767-2455.

Family Fun Day, Kelowna
Last Sunday of May at Parkinson Recreation Centre, Harvey and Spall. For 18 years this has been one of the great family events of the year. There is enough going on to keep pre-teen children amused from noon to 4 p.m. Tons of games, draws, prizes, competitions and awards. Also entertainment, activity tents and play areas, both indoors and out. And it's all free. 860-3938, ext. 151.

World Vision Fun Run
Usually the last Saturday of the month but sometimes first Saturday of June. A decade-old event. Choice of a 5- or 10-kilometre run (3 or 6 miles) or a 5-kilometre (3-mile) walk. Takes place on the Mission Creek Greenway, Kelowna. 862-3511.

Okanagan International Children's Festival, Penticton
Penticton Community Centre, last weekend of May. 490-2426,
1-800-663-1900, www.okchildrensfest.org.

June

Oyama Fun Day, Oyama
First weekend of June. Pancake breakfast, parade, silent auction,
children's field events and a dunk tank. 717-7756.

Kayak Rodeo
Early June weekend. On the Shuswap River below the Kingfisher
ball park, 31 kilometres (19 miles) east of Enderby. Auction, dinner,
entertainment and races. 838-0761.

Taste of Japan
Kelowna, first Friday and Saturday of June, at the Performance
Centre, Kasugai Gardens, City Hall lawn and other sites. Japanese
food, arts, sports and culture celebrate Kelowna's ties with its sister
city, Kasugai, Japan. www.kelownakasugai.com.

Children's Festival
Vernon's Polson Park, in the afternoon on a Sunday in early June.
542-3121, ext. 103.

Summerland Action Festival
Summerland, early June weekend at Dale Meadows Complex and
other locations. A parade, Giant's Head Run, Man of Steel Triathlon
and slo-pitch tournament. 494-2686.

Pow Wow
Osoyoos, mid-June, at Nk'Mip Resort. Native dancers and drummers
from all over North America entertain and compete for prizes.
495-7279.

Creative Chaos Craft Fair, Vernon
Second week of June. One of the biggest craft displays in the Valley with
more than 200 artists showing and selling their wares. Also specialty
foods, outdoor creative activities, local performing arts talent and
Students' Showcase. Vernon Recreation Centre, 545-6963.

Air Affair
Hosted by Shuswap Flying Club at Salmon Arm Airport every
Father's Day. Displays of helicopters, ultra-lights, para gliders and
other planes, plus a flea market, trade show and pancake breakfast.
675-4895.

Peach City Beach Cruise, Penticton

Third week of June. A three-day antique and classic car and motor-cycle convention with more than 700 restored vehicles lined up along the road next to Okanagan Lake. Concessions, entertainment, dance. www. peach citybeachcruise.com.

Paddle Festival

Gay and Lesbian Pride Week

Starts mid-June with events in various Okanagan locations. The focus is in Kelowna. The week includes a film festival, talent show, swim party, softball tournament and cruise on the Fintry Queen. Honoured is Homopogo, a gay relative of Ogopogo.

Paddle Festival, Summerland

Powell Beach, mid-June week-end. The Okanagan Paddle Festival features races, displays and demos of kayaks, canoes and outriggers. Admission is free. There is a charge to try out the boats. 862-8049.

Gold Wing Can Am Rally and Mountain Light-up

mid-June, Osoyoos. The highlight is the stream of brightly lighted Honda motorcycles twisting down Anarchist Mountain after sunset. 495-7142.

Aboriginal Day

June 21. Buffalo burger BBQs, dancing, craft displays, stories and music are presented by First Nations throughout the Valley. In Salmon Arm at the Switsemalph Learning Centre, in Vernon at the Friendship Centre, in Kelowna at Ki-Low-Na Friendship Society, in Penticton at Okanagan Lake Park and in Osoyoos at the Nk'Mip Desert Centre. 1-800-990-2432.

Sunshine Festival

held mid-month in downtown Vernon, is billed as one of the largest sidewalk sales in British Columbia. Up to 10,000 people fill the streets for music, merchandise, adventure demonstrations and lots of food.

Funtastic Sports tournament

Vernon, Armstrong, Enderby and Lumby. June through July 1 week-end. Competitions in slo-pitch, golf, soccer, beach volleyball and lawn bowling as well as live musical performances. 558-7756, www.funtastic.org.

Mayor's Environmental Expo
Kelowna, early June, City Park. Demonstrations of cycling, effic-ient fireplaces, forest resources and other friendly and efficient energy savers. 868-2768.

Pacific Northwest Elvis Festival and Friends of Elvis Festival
Penticton and Osoyoos, end of June. Car show, fireworks, and a festival with a gathering of people with Elvis connections, Elvis look-alikes and Elvis sound-alikes. Three days at Queen's Park and the Trade and Convention Centre in Penticton and Gyro Park, Osoyoos. 492-3584, 1-800-663-5052, www.pentictonelvisfestival.com.

Shakespeare
For a dozen years, Shakespeare Kelowna has been presenting the Bard. Plays are at the Island Stage in Kelowna's Waterfront Park, running from the last week of June through the first week of July. www.shakespearekelowna.org.

Jack Brow track meet
Apple Bowl, Kelowna, last weekend in June. 1,200 athletes from all over North America compete in track and field. 491-1384, ext.104.

July
Canada Day
Every community celebrates Canada's 1867 confederation on July 1, and events often spill over to the closest weekend. A fireworks display usually ends the day. In Kelowna events centre around Waterfront Park with entertainment at the Island Stage and Prospera Place. At Gyro Park in Penticton there are 12 hours of continuous entertainment with a dog show and birthday cake. Westside Daze in Westbank is a big one with dozens of events over three days. Osoyoos has a Cherry Festival at Gyro Beach. In Lake Country there is a lot for kids to do at Beasley Park, including a pancake breakfast, games and a root beer garden.

Rally in the Valley
in Peachland and Kelowna. First weekend in July. A gathering of up to 350 vintage British sports cars and motorcycles. Beach Ave. in Peachland is closed at midday Saturday for viewing. Other events centre around Kelowna's Ramada Inn and Grand Hotel. www.obcc.ca/ritv.

Guisachan Garden flower show

first weekend in July, Kelowna, at Guisachan Heritage Park, Cameron Ave. Guest speakers, craft show, plant sales, entertainment, demonstration garden, flower show and judging. Put on by the Central Okanagan Heritage Society. 861-7188.

Highland Games

Penticton, early July, King's Park. Sports events, pipe band competition and Scottish highland dancing. 1-800-663-5052.

Mainstage Festival

Penticton and Summerland, 10 days of theatre in early July. This provincial drama festival is hosted by Summerland Singers and Players and features the "best of" from 10 drama zones. Mainstage has run for 70 years. 494-1931. www.theatrebc.org/mainstage.

Extreme Sports Wakefest

features wakeboarding, early July weekend at Kelowna's Waterfront Park. Professional competition with freestyle, skating, hydrofoil and other events including bikini judging. Rock concerts in the evening. www.extremesports series.ca.

Kelowna International Regatta

At City Park and various downtown locations, mid-July. This weekend festival incorporates the Classic and Antique Boat Show, boat building, wakeboarding, water skiing and a swim race. 860-0529, www.kelownaregatta.com.

Skateboard Competition

at Westside Skate Park, Westbank, on a Saturday afternoon in mid-July. Categories include novice, trick, advanced and girls only. Live DJ, food, pro demonstrations and prizes. 768-3378.

Summerland Rodeo Days

two days, mid-July weekend at Summerland Rodeo Grounds. Billed as "the biggest little rodeo in the South Okanagan," with eight major events plus children's events during intermissions. 494-2686.

Cowboy Campfire

Canyon Creek Ranch, Osoyoos, mid-July. Held for 13 years. Campfires, sing-alongs, gold panning, horse riding, poetry, BBQ. 446-2455, www.canyoncreekranch.ca.

Who are the Pawns in this Game?

Kelowna has close to 20, Penticton has 6, and Vernon, 5. By comparison, there are only 18 listed for Vancouver and less than a dozen in Greater Toronto.

We are not enumerating art galleries, museums, bookstores or even theatres. We are talking about an entirely different cultural icon, one that makes just as distinctive a mark on the surrounding landscape — pawnshops.

While local Tourist Information Centres are keen to promote the Valley's golf courses, ski hills and wineries nothing is said about the Okanagan being the pawn shop capital of Canada, perhaps even the western hemisphere.

The profitable part of the pawn business comes from making loans, not from selling merchandise. Imagine it's Wednesday night and there won't be another paycheque for two days. The kids are crying for dinner, the spouse is saying that it's time the two of you went out for a drink and your burly buddy next door wants the 20 bucks he loaned you.

Some people have a wad of plastic, a line of credit at the

CONTINUES ON PAGE 149

Rodeo

at Salmon Arm Fair Grounds, Saturday evening and Sunday afternoon in mid-July with bull riding, saddle bronc, bareback and barrel racing events. 833-4031.

Mozart Festival

at various locations in Kelowna. Outdoor concerts at the Island Stage, performances at Summerhill Winery, lunchtime in the park and children's performances. 762-3747, www.okanaganmozartfestival.com.

Fat Cat Children's Festival

Saturday, late July, City Park, Kelowna. One month after Family Fun Day comes another great free event for kids. It starts at noon with a multitude of booths offering games, demonstrations and samples. Also a climbing wall, First Nations' crafts, races, contests, face painting and balloons. Admission is free and the $4 Booster Packs, which have samples from retailers and manufacturers, sell out quickly. About 15,000 attend this festival that has run since 1991. 763-3212, www.fatcatfestival.ca.

Beach Blanket Film Festival

Penticton, on the east side of Lakeside Resort, third weekend in July, three evenings starting at 10 p.m. Canadian films are projected on a full-size screen floating on Okanagan Lake. For a dozen years audiences of up to 1,000 curl up on beach blankets under a starry sky and enjoy the show. 490-4969, www.beachblanketfilmfest.ca.

Triathlon

Penticton, third weekend. The Boston Pizza Junior Triathlon is held on Saturday and the Peach Classic Triathlon, Olympic distance, on Sunday. Both events start with a swim in Okanagan Lake. 1-800-663-5052, www.wi.ca/peach.

August

Awesome Summer Nite, Kelowna

At the foot of Bernard Ave. near *The Sails* sculpture, from 3 to 9 p.m., Saturday, near the end of the month. Hundreds of antique and collector cars, trucks and motorcycles. Live 1950s and 1960s entertainment. No admission charge. 862-3515.

Naramata August Faire

First holiday Monday in August at the community park. The fair features entertainment, crafts, arts, games, food, a parade and family events. 1-800-663-5052.

bank, stocks in Nortel and an ATM down the street. But not everyone has access to instant cash, so try to put yourself in the picture.

You might just grab the kids' TV and a few DVDs, march down to the local pawnshop, plunk the goods on the counter and mumble, "How much?"

The friendly proprietor would examine the goods and shoot back, "Fifty bucks." Pawnshops generally give about half of what items are worth. You do the paperwork and head to the grocery store.

Two weeks later you reach for your *Night of the Living Dead* DVD and remember the pawnshop. You slap your receipt on the counter and tell the still-friendly proprietor you want your stuff back.

"That'll be $65," he says. You hand over the money and an assistant appears with your TV and movies. That $50 loan cost you $15. While that might seem horrendous — 30 percent interest for 15 days, or 660 percent per annum — it isn't that simple. The interest is more likely to be $5. The other $10 is a charge for storage and paperwork. Maximum loan period is 30 days, but, unlike most loans, this is one you don't have to pay back. If you never claim your property the items will be put up for sale.

Cowboy Festival
O'Keefe Ranch, Vernon. First weekend in August. The cowboy way of life is celebrated with poetry, music, a rodeo, dog demonstrations and a Wild West show. 542-7868, www. okeeferanch.bc.ca.

Cherryville Festival of the Arts
early August weekend. At the Community Hall and Hanson Park in this small community, east of Vernon, with transportation between the two locations provided by a wagon ride. Music, performing arts, food fair, market, healing arts, demonstrations and children's activities. 545-0771.

Square Dancing
Penticton, second week of August. For 50 years up to 2,000 dancers have converged on King's Park in Penticton to swing their partners for five days. 1-800-663-5052.

Mardi Gras Street Festival, Kelowna
Second weekend of August. Bernard Ave. closes to vehicles and opens to a Saturday morning arcade, sidewalk sale, 100 vendor booths, family fun activities and entertainment. There are also carnival rides, cherry fair and dogs catching Frisbees. The event covers six city blocks and has three stages with live entertainment. 862-3515, www.downtownkelowna.com.

Skaha Lake Ultra Swim
Saturday, mid-month. A 12-kilometre (7-mile) swim the length of Skaha Lake, from Penticton's Muscle Beach, to Okanagan Falls. Has been run for two decades.
www.ultraswimcanada.com.

Kelowna Blues Festival
Not to be confused with the Salmon Arm event a week later, this one-day, eight-hour, Sunday singsong takes place at City Park from 1:30 to 9:30 p.m. 868-3307, www.parksalive.com.

Salmon Arm Roots and Blues Festival
Four stages are set up in this Shuswap community for an eclectic mixture of music from around the world. Runs Friday through Sunday in mid-August. Includes many daytime and kid-friendly events with the headliner stage running from 5 to 11 p.m. 833-4096, www.rootsandblues.ca.

Penticton Peachfest
second week of August. Five days of family entertainment including

sand castle building, concerts, parade, pancake breakfast and the crowning of Miss Penticton. This festival has been running for more than 55 years and there are plenty of ripe, juicy peaches just off the trees. 492-4103, www.peach fest.com.

Apple Triathlon
Kelowna, third weekend of August at the Apple Bowl and surrounding area. Kids of Steel, Applecore and Appleseed races take place before the main event. With close to 600 competitors, this is the second biggest triathlon in B.C. The biggest follows this one, in Penticton. www.appletriathlon.com.

Subaru Ironman Canada Triathlon
Monday at the end of August. The biggest event of the year for Penticton, involving 1,700 athletes plus coaches, friends and sponsors from 30 countries. Roughly 4,500 locals volunteer. Having surpassed 20 years it is the oldest Ironman race in continental North America and features the largest single-wave swim start in Ironman history (1,785 athletes). The swim is 3.8 kilometres (2.4 miles), the bike ride is 179 kilometres (111 miles) and the run is 42.4 kilometres (26.75 miles). It takes a champion athlete just to finish. www.ironman.ca.

Kinsmen Pro Rodeo
Takes place over the weekend in late August at the Oliver Rodeo Grounds. 497-6934.

Interior Provincial Exhibition and Stampede
Known commonly as the Armstrong Fair, this is a huge annual agricultural fair. Features heavy and light horses, a four-day CPRA rodeo, a parade and the largest midway outside of Vancouver. Attendance is close to 90,000 and many rodeo events sell out. It is a five-day fair at the end of August and has been operating for more than 105 years. 546-9406, www.armstrongbc.com/ipe.

Festival of the Tomato
Oliver, afternoon of the last day of September at Covent Farms. Feature of the event is the head-to-head tomato fight. Also entertainment and tomato-based food. 498-6321.

September
Wiggle Waggle Walkathon
To raise money for the SPCA, pet owners gather at Mission Creek Regional Park, Kelowna, on the first Sunday of the month, with their pedestrian pets, for a leisurely stroll. 861-1515.

Artwalk

Lake Country's display of quilts, paintings, sculptures, and other works of art runs all day for two days on the first weekend in September at the Lake Country Community Complex in Winfield. 766-1485.

Penticton Dragon Boat Festival

Saturday and Sunday mornings in early September, a prelude to the bigger Kelowna event. The 20 paddlers per boat race 500 metres (550 yards) from Penticton Marina on Okanagan Lake, parallel to the beach, to the dock in front of Lakeside Resort. 1-888-309-5674, www.prcc. bc.ca/dragonboat.

Summerland Agricultural Fair

First weekend in September, Summerland Arena. Local arts, crafts and crops. This fall fair is into its 95th year. 494-2686.

Peachland Fall Fair

One of the smaller autumn festivals. First weekend in September. 767-2218.

Pentastic Jazz Festival

Early September, Penticton. Jazz and Dixieland bands from all over North America perform at four locations. A shuttle bus is available for those not wanting to walk between events. All venues provide seating and dancing facilities and the *S.S. Sicamous*, Penticton's historic paddlewheeler, is set up for performances. Free performance Sunday at Gyro Park. www.pentasticjazz.com.

Salmon Arm Fall Fair

Mid-September for three days at the fairgrounds next to Blackburn Park. More than 106 years old. Saturday morning parade through Salmon Arm. The fair features local arts and crafts, farm animal competitions, midway and commercial exhibits, 832-0442, 1-877-725-6667.

Kelowna Dragon Boat Festival

The big boats with 20 paddlers, a drummer and a helmsperson race for three days, mid-September, at Waterfront Park, Kelowna. The second biggest dragon boat festival in B.C. involves 150 teams and 3,500 participants. 1-888-309-5674, 868-1136, www.kelownadragonboatfestival.com.

Terry Fox Run

Kelowna. Up to 900 runners, walkers and cyclists raise money for

Dragon Boat Festival

cancer research in mid-September. Starts at Mission sports field on Gordon Dr. www.terryfoxrun.org.

Kelowna AIDS Walk,
Waterfront Park, Saturday in mid-September. A walk to raise money to support persons with AIDS. Registration at 10 a.m., walk at 11 a.m. Food, awards and prizes in early afternoon.

Field Of Dreams car show
Kelowna City Park, mid-September weekend, auction and car show with more than 1,000 exotic and antique cars. 769-7913.

EnRoot Harvest and Heritage Festival
Penticton, Saturday, mid-September, Gyro Park. An extension of the Farmers' Market celebrates the work of farmers and growers. Displays by the Society for Creative Anachronism. 1-800-663-5052.

Nk'Mip Salmon Bake Festival
Osoyoos, end of September. Fresh salmon is baked over an open pit and accompanied by traditional Native entertainers and locally brewed beers and wines. At Nk'Mip Resort Community Hall. 495-3366.

East Kelowna Fall Fair
McCullough Rd., Friday to Sunday on the last weekend of September. Parade, craft show, horticultural exhibits, orchard tours, wine tasting, entertainment and a dance. www.eastkelownafallfair.com.

October
Run for the Cure
in support of breast cancer research, first Sunday in October, at Waterfront Park, Kelowna. More than 2,000 participants run 5 kilometres (3 miles). 1-800-561-6111, www. cbcf.org.

Harvest Pumpkin Festival and Giant Pumpkin Weigh-in
downtown Armstrong. Early October, in its fourth year. The pumpkin catapult, pumpkin carving and pumpkin light-up are the highlights. The walls next to the railway tracks that run through the middle of town are lined with carved lighted pumpkins. The town hopes to set a world record for most pumpkins on a wall. 546-8155.

Chamber Music Kelowna
starts its series in early October, in the Mary Irwin Theatre at the Rotary Centre for the Arts. In its 25th year.
www.chambermusickelowna.ca.

Okanagan International Marathon
plus a half-marathon and a 10-kilometre (6-mile) race. Kelowna, Sunday, mid-month, 7:30 a.m. City Park. The 42.2-kilometre (26.75-mile) run attracts 2,500 participants. 762-0665.

Apple Fair
Up to 20 varieties of apples are available for tasting and touching. Recipes and juice are handed out while pies, candy apples and apples themselves are for sale. At the Orchard Museum in the Laurel Building, 1304 Ellis St., Kelowna, in late October. 861-1515.

November
Summerland Festival of Lights
end of November. The downtown light-up kicks off the Christmas season on the last Friday of the month. 494-2686.

December
Light-Up
Most communities have a Christmas light-up ceremony the first Friday or Saturday in December. In Kelowna the Christmas Light-up takes place from Towne Centre Mall on Bernard Ave. to Kerry Park on the lakeshore. Penticton has a parade at the start of December. Osoyoos has Christmas Light-up, Santa's Workshop, Downtown Open House, Town Light-up Parade, prizes, entertainment and a wind-up bonfire.

OKANOGAN, WASHINGTON CALENDAR OF EVENTS

(The river and the Valley are named Okanogan as is the town of Okanogan, about halfway down the Valley.)

All Okanogan, Washington phone numbers use the 509 area code.

May

Pacific Rail Car Operators
Oroville. A celebration of the two-man pump handle rail cars at the Depot Museum in mid-month. 476-2739.

Tonasket Rodeo
Last weekend in May. 486-4429.

Farmers' Market
Okanogan (town), May to October. Tuesday afternoons and Saturday mornings, Legion Park, Harley St., 826-1259.

June

Farmers' Market
Tonasket, June to October. Late Thursday afternoons, University Place Farmers Market, 3617 Bridgeport Way.

Tonasket Founder's Day Rodeo
Beginning of June. 486-4543.

Okanogan Days
Main Street Celebration. Town of Okanogan in mid-June. Torchlight parade, street dance, street fair, parade, farmers' market, live music, vendors and food court. 422-5525.

Molson Mid-Summer Fest
June 21 at the Molson Ghost Town, near Oroville.

July

Independence Day
July 4 celebrations are held in most communities, with fireworks ending the festivities. Oroville has Oroville Days with boat races. Brewster has a parade and car show. 476-2739.

Can-Am Apple Cup Hydro Boat Races
Oroville, mid-July, at Deep Bay, Lake Osoyoos. 476-2739.

August
International Apple Bin Boat Regatta
Deep Bay Park, mid-August, Oroville. Boats made out of apple bins are paddled across the bay.

Omak Stampede
Four days in early August. Rodeo, carnival, suicide ride, dance, demolition derby and live entertainment. In the World Famous Suicide Race, horses and riders charge down a cliff and into a river. www.omakstampede.org.

Okanogan River Garlic Festival
Late August, Tonasket History Park. Live music, arts and crafts and tasting of some of the 120 varieties of garlic grown in the Okanogan Valley. 486-1395, www. filareefarm.com.

September
County Fair
Early September, Okanogan, 175 Rodeo Trail Dr.

OKANAGAN LITE:
Finding Home

The Interstate, heading north from Portland, Oregon, is hardly a holiday treat, and after you conquer the countless bridges, cross the state line and enter Washington, things get worse. The claustrophobia tightens as you file through a flat, featureless corridor shadowed by stumpy shrubs and truncated trees whose growth has been stunted by decades of exhaust fumes. Bland billboards sprout at pavement's edge.

The twisted turnpikes of Seattle threaten the trepid traveller with a spidery web of pavement waiting to entomb the unwary fly. Seattle spiders spin their traps with a maze of interchanges that have the frenzied navigator shouting frantic instructions.

One wrong turn, a missed turnoff, a mechanical failure, a tire gone limp, or a mishap with another frightened driver and the spider will suck the financial lifeblood from you. Dry roadside carcasses attest to that.

Somewhere after the international border the web weakens; but it is not until after Abbotsford, B.C. has shrunk in the rear-view mirror that the last elastic strand of the sticky web stretches to its limit and snaps. You are free, and cities with promising names like Hope and Merritt offer encouragement as the countryside opens into the visual panorama that infused you with the joy of travelling in the first place. Traffic thins, and you roll eastward, rising and falling on gentle hills like a ship bobbing on the ocean. The vista encompasses hundreds of kilometres and your eyes feel like they are suddenly free from a life sentence in a visual prison. The huge and open sky reminds you of the prairies, and pristine snow powders the mountaintops where noisy snowmobiles never tread.

On verdant hillsides contented cows seem to smirk as they munch fresh green shoots, knowing, perhaps, that their lot is to provide milk and cheese and not the fodder for bland burger joints.

The radio again provides CBC's poignant chatter between intelligent people, and the music does not repeat itself every three seconds. The road winds into a valley where sailboats play on a lake and orchards and vineyards pattern the hillsides. You stop for gas and fill up without anyone questioning your honesty and requiring payment in advance. You unfold a map and the Okanagan is the name they give to this place. It feels like home.

The Okanagan that summer
tourists don't see

4 FOR MORE iNFORMATiON

THE CURIOUS TRAVELLER ALWAYS HAS QUESTIONS TO ASK. Answers, fortunately, are often as close as the person walking down the street — as long that person isn't also a tourist with questions of their own. There is no need to be shy in the Okanagan. The residents are friendly, somewhat laid back and more than willing to answer a question or two.

For detailed information on specific subjects, check out the books listed next. They are generally available in bookstores and specialty shops. For maps, lists of accommodation, campgrounds and restaurants go to the tourist information centres listed below. They are particularly generous with brochures on wineries and winery tours.

BOOKS
Cycling
Cycling the Kettle Valley Railway, Dan and Sandra Lanford,
    Rocky Mountain Books
Kelowna Cycling Map, distributed free in bike shops by the Kelowna Cycling
    Coalition
Okanagan Cycling Trails, William Rosenthal and Greg Winter
South Slopes Map — Routes of Kelowna's Crawford Estates, printed by
    Kelowna Mountain Bike Club

Gardening
Gardening in the Dry Interior of B.C., editor Anne Ginns,
    Okanagan Past and Present Society

Golf
Okanagan Golf Points of View, Sheila Paynter

Hiking/Nature
Hiking Trails Enjoyed by The Vernon Outdoors Club, published by the Vernon
    Outdoors Club
Okanagan Trips and Trails, Judie Steeves and Murphy Shewchuk, Sonotek
    Publishing
Plants of the Southern Interior, Ministry of Forests and Lone Pine Publishing

Tracks, Trails and Naturalists' Tales, Alice Hargreaves, Central Okanagan
    Naturalists' Club

History

A Rich and Fruitful Land, Harbour Publishing

Camp Vernon: A Century of Canadian Military History, Hugh Rayment and
    Patrick Sherlock, Kettle Valley Publishing

Fintry: Lives, Loves and Dreams, Stan Sauerwein, Trafford Publishing

Okanagan History: Report of the Okanagan Historical Society, published by
    the Society, 2003 annual edition was the 67th

Okanagan Roots, Doug Cox, Skookum Publications

Q'Sapi: A History of Okanagan Peoples, Shirley Louise, Theytus Books

Kettle Valley Railway

Canadian Pacific's Kettle Valley Railway, Joe Smuin, British Railway Modellers
    of North America

Kettle Valley Railway Mileboards, Joe Smuin, North Kildonan Press

Kettle Valley Railway: Railways of Western Canada, Gerry Doeksen

McCulloch's Wonder: The Story of the Kettle Valley Railway, Barrie Sanford,
    Whitecap Books

Steam on the Kettle Valley, Robert D. Turner, Sono Nis Press

Steel Rails and Iron Men, Barrie Sanford, Whitecap Books

Map Books

Backroad Mapbook Vol. III, Kamloops Okanagan. Mussio Ventures

Fishing B.C., Okanagan, Mussio Ventures

Motor Touring

Back Roads: Southern Interior, Lone Pine Publishing

*Destination Highways—A Motorcycle Enthusiast's Guide to the Best 185 Roads
    in Southern B.C.*, Twisted Edge Publishing

More Tours Made Easy: Discover Okanagan, Nicola and Boundary, published
    by Alice Lundy and Dorothy Zoellner

Four-Wheeling in the B.C. Interior, published by Mark Bestwick

Ogopogo

In Search of Ogopogo, Arlene Gaal, Hancock House Publishing

Ogopogo: The Misunderstood Lake Monster, Don Levers, Sandhill Publishing

Okanagan Mountain Fire

Firestorm: the Summer B.C. Burned, Ross Freake & Don Plant, McLelland &
    Stewart

Okanagan Mountain Fire: A Time of Unity, Andrew Millar and April Crawford
    Brown, Tiger Marketing

Wildfire, Charles Anderson and Lori Culbert, Greystone Books

Picture Books

A Journey Through the Okanagan, Natural Color Productions
Beauty is ... a Collection of Okanagan Art, Cyndi Krueger, Summer Springs
    Publications
Okanagan, British Columbia's Golden Triangle, Josef Hanus, JH Fine Art
    Photo Ltd.
Okanagan Scenic Guide, Natural Color Productions
The Okanagan, Tanya Lloyd, Whitecap Books

Rocks and Climbing

Geology of the Kelowna Area, Murray Roed, Kelowna Geology Committee.
    Look for a second printing of this excellent book.
Rockclimbs: Kelowna and Area, published and written by Dean Urness
Skaha Rockclimbs, Howie Richardson, Elaho Publishing

Wine

British Columbia Wine Country, John Schreiner, Kevin Miller, Whitecap Books
Wineries of British Columbia, revised 2004, John Schreiner, Whitecap Books

TOURIST INFORMATION CENTRES

All Okanagan, B.C. phone numbers use the 250 area code.

Area Information

Thompson Okanagan Tourism Association,
1332 Water St., Kelowna, B.C., V1Y 9P4. 860-5999,
www.thompsonokanagan.com

Okanagan Connector Visitor Info Centre
(located on the highway from Merritt),
Hwy. 97C, Peachland, Westbank, V4T 2G3. 767-6677

Okanagan, B.C. Cities

Armstrong Chamber of Commerce
3550 Bridge St., Armstrong, V0E 1B0. 546-8155

Enderby Chamber of Commerce
700 Railway Ave., Enderby, V0E 1V0. 838-6727, 1-877-213-6509

Kelowna Chamber of Commerce
44 Harvey Ave., Kelowna, V1Y 6C9. 861-1515, 1-800-663-4345

Lake Country Visitor Info
15686 Hwy. 97, 548-3776

Lumby Chamber of Commerce
2400 Vernon St., Lumby, V0E 2G0. 547-2300

Oliver and District Travel
36205 93rd St., Oliver, V0H 1T0. 498-6321

Osoyoos Visitor Info Centre
Hwy. 3 & Hwy. 97. Box 500, V0H 1V0. 495-3366, 1-888-676-9667

Okanagan, B.C. Cities (continued)

Peachland Museum Visitor Info
5812 Beach Ave., Peachland, V0H 1X0. 767-2455

Penticton Info Centre
888 Westminster Ave. W., Penticton, V2A 8S2. 493-4055, 1-800-663-4103

Salmon Arm Visitor Info Centre
1-751 Marine Park Dr. N.E., Salmon Arm, V1E 2W7. 832-6247, 1-877-725-6667

Summerland Chamber of Commerce
15600 Hwy. 9, Summerland, V0H 1Z0. 494-2686

Vernon (2 locations)
Watson House, 701 Hwy. 97 S., 542-1415, 1-800-665-0795, and,
6326 Hwy. 97 N., Vernon, V1T 6M4. 545-2959

Westbank Visitor Info Centre
Unit # 4 – 2375 Pamela Rd., Westbank, V4T 2H9. 768-3378, 1-866-768-3378

Washington

All Okanogan, Washington phone numbers use the 509 area code.

Brewster Chamber of Commerce
Box 1087, WA 98812, 923-2393

Okanogan Chamber of Commerce
Box 1125, WA 98840, 422-5525

Omak Chamber of Commerce
401 Omak Ave., WA 98841, 826-1880

Oroville Visitor Information
1730 Main St., WA 98844, 476-2739

Tonasket Chamber of Commerce
Box 523, WA 98855, 486-4429

INDEX